Making Glove Puppets

MAKING GLOVE PUPPETS

Esmé McLaren

Boston   PLAYS, INC.   Publishers

© ESMÉ MCLAREN 1973

Published by G. Bell & Sons Ltd, London

First American edition published by
Plays. Inc.
1973

Library of Congress Catalog Card No. 73–1573
ISBN: 0–8238–0144–6

Printed in Great Britain

Contents

The Finger Stalls

Embroidery Stitches for Garments

PUPPETS

Introduction

This book describes in simple terms, fully detailed, the processes to be followed in making glove puppets.

It is easily comprehended and adequately illustrated.

Full size patterns are provided from which tracings can be made direct from the book page, and the related pattern placing charts ensure economy of materials (with a thought for the stroke of the fur fabric pile where necessary).

Experienced makers will not be offended by the fullness of the descriptions, diagrams and illustrations given, as they will appreciate that some workers prefer to follow descriptions and others depend on the drawings.

These puppets are not 'theatrical' in the full sense, that is, specially made for performances before a large audience, although of course, this is possible, but puppets for this purpose are usually accentuated in features and often artistically grotesque to achieve a desired effect at a distance. This requires a special approach not called for here.

The puppets in this book are adequate in every way for school and home use, and of course for family gatherings, and basically there are four types of designs included, suitable for these purposes. Several puppets are given in two sizes, approximately 13 inches and 10 inches in height, so that small, as well as larger hands can use them.

Another special feature is that most of these puppets can be used 'in their own right' as cuddly toys.

In addition it is possible to attach other heads and feet to the 'gloves' and it should be mentioned that the author's *The Craft of Stuffed Toys* included several which could be attached in the same way, including the Poodle, Lamb and Rabbit designs. This book also contained reliable methods for enlarging and diminishing patterns, offering opportunities for even smaller or between sizes if required.

Several variations of the finger-stall shape, size and design are given to cope with individual tastes.

Various designs and suggestions are given for clothes and accessories, most of which are sufficiently simple in style for children to make them themselves and so share in the production of their playthings. Some suggestions for the use of embroidery, suitable to decorate small garments, are also given and illustrated.

This book opens a wide field of imaginative designs for glove puppets and is an invitation to inspire those interested to design and make their own glove puppets.

Technical Information

MATERIALS

Apart from the costumes and garments, the main materials used for the puppets are fur fabrics and felt. Small pieces of leather—a soft, glossy finished gloving leather—are needed for such parts as noses, etc., where a shiny surface is required.

Fur fabrics are an extensive group of materials in many qualities, types and shades which are most suitable to imitate animals' coats. Expensive ones need not be used as many pieces are obtainable as remnants or in economy bundles. Turnings, normally of $\frac{1}{4}$ inch width are required for the seams. This is a material which can be successfully washed. It can also be dyed if a particular colour is not otherwise obtainable in the texture desired. It is made in wool and man-made fibres.

Felt is easy to manipulate and makes a good contrast with fur fabrics. It is obtainable in many shades of all colours, and generally needs no turnings. In some cases where only a very thin quality of felt can be purchased it is recommended that it should be backed with Iron-on Vilene especially where it has to be stuffed. This will help to prevent alteration of the shape and size beyond that which the pattern requires, and will strengthen thin felts.

Dress materials. It is usually found that such small garments as those needed for puppets are best chosen from the smaller patterned designs for children's clothes, and often pieces left from home dressmaking can be used for this purpose which will further delight the recipient who may have a dress of the same material.

Tarlatan. This is a useful material of some stiffness and should be chosen for such items as the ruffs, etc., where a stiffened material is a necessity.

Iron-on Vilene is a modern product which is of great value in giving more body to softer materials or thin felts, where this is needed, especially when felts have to be stuffed. It is applied to the back of the materials (see page 19).

SEAMS AND EDGES

On small articles such as glove puppets where seams in length and width are reduced in size, hand sewing is much easier to do, and has rather more elasticity than machine work. The advantage of the former is obvious where the seams have to take the extra strain of the insertion of stuffing. Hand sewing also permits more variety of stitches. It is an advantage to sew by hand when two different types of materials such as felt and fur fabrics are joined. Where three or four thicknesses of materials occur, it will be necessary to stab the hand stitching along the seam to prevent a bias and to be certain that all the pieces of materials are included as the seam progresses.

Cotton garments can be machine sewn and the bindings put on by a machine attachment, if so desired, but it is not essential—hand sewing can be just as strong and neat.

TURNINGS

Usually the seams on felt are on the inside and as near the edge as possible—no turnings are then required. On fur fabrics $\frac{1}{4}$ inch turnings are added to the outline round the template while cutting out. The stitching is worked just along the inside of the marking out line.

Fur fabric turnings can also be oversewn after the seams are completed. If they are exactly the same width, the oversewing can be done first, before the seam is stitched. The cotton garments are usually made up with French seams for which a $\frac{1}{4}$ inch turning is given, resulting in an $\frac{1}{8}$ inch seam. Some of the edges such as necks, armholes, and openings can be made attractive and secure with the addition of a thin bias binding, in this case no turnings are needed. Hems require larger turnings as indicated on the patterns, and should be sewn by one of the invisible methods now used in dressmaking.

THREADS

There are several types and varieties of sewing threads which suitably combine the strength and fineness needed for the strong seam work on puppets. The usual sewing cottons can be used as a single thread if sufficiently strong or as doubled threads if the strength is doubtful, more especially on fur fabrics. In addition, man-made fibres on reels are strong and the best varieties are recommended. For some purposes thick thread is needed and Anchor soft embroidery cotton or similar thick embroidery threads should be used. Of this size and texture they are suitable to indicate various parts in the finishes of a puppet. Mouth lines and marks to show the divisions of paws, etc., can be worked in this thickness of thread. Use a matching sewing cotton for all seams unless otherwise stated. It is advisable to start and end with a good size knot to make both ends of seams very secure.

NEEDLES AND PINS

An assortment of needles is always useful, though the type preferred by the worker can be chosen for all seamwork. The size is governed by the thickness of the materials and thread. Very thick pointed needles are often needed such as No. 15 darners. These have their special use in pricking perforations on the card templates large enough to pass through the fine point of a pencil to make the dotted lines on the back of the materials—usually position lines. This type of needle is also convenient to use when easing stuffing into position by passing the point through the covering material and gently moving the filling where required. A double long darning needle for the insertion of eyes and crewel needles for embroidery thread will also be needed.

It is advisable to use pins with coloured heads which are fine, sharp and easily found in fur fabrics. It is better to use them at right angles to the edge of the seam to avoid puckering or forming a bias on the materials. It is most essential first to pin at the start and end of each seam, and then between at frequent intervals. If this is done the materials will fit together evenly and many seams can be stitched without tacking. Hat pins are valuable aids to keep the filling in place while stuffing heads, etc., as they are long enough to pass through from one side to the other and can be re-inserted as the stuffing progresses.

TOOLS AND ACCESSORIES

In addition to a well equipped sewing box the following tools, etc., are essential for the making up of the puppets:

Scissors. Good cutting-out scissors, especially on felt, will be required, of a size most comfortable for the worker to handle and control the materials. Curved scissors are also most helpful for small rounded parts.

Hat pins. Small 3–4 inch hat pins are most useful to keep filling in place while stuffing is in progress.

Round-nosed pliers and cutters. Either as separate tools or a pair of milliner's pliers, combining both of these tools, these are necessary for preparing glass or perspex eyes on wire and for cutting the pipe cleaners.

Stuffing sticks. Various types are obtainable, some of which are little more than a plain piece of dowel rod. A good stuffing stick with the operative end flattened to a wedge shape surface and ending in a 'V' cut as shown in Diagram 1 will be the most useful aid to successful stuffing, the object being the easy insertion of the stuffing material, which is carried down by the 'V' notch without damage and stretching of the covering material—especially if it is thin felt. Where required, this shaped stick will also allow small additional amounts of stuffing to be passed between the outer covering and the main quantity of stuffing material already inserted to improve contours, and be withdrawn easily without bringing back any of the filling. A smaller stuffing stick of similar shape is most useful for small pointed sections of the work but will probably have to be made from a wooden skewer or even a blunt orange stick.

A thimble and a tape measure

A comb is useful to raise the pile of fur fabrics and to groom finished puppets in this material.

Sheets of thin card suitable for pattern templates.

Pencils. Dark marking pencils which do not require as much pressure on materials and used lightly, will not leave a trail of graphite to soil the fabrics, are recommended (3B or 4B).

Tailor's chalk instead of or as well as pencils can be used for marking out. This type of chalk can also be obtained in pencil form as well as flat pieces.

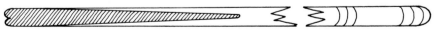

1 *Wedge shape stuffing stick, 9 ins. in length*

BACK STITCHING

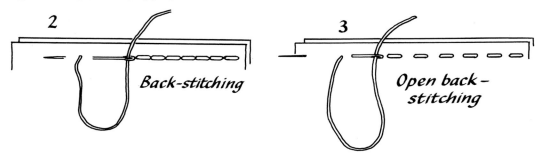

Back-stitching

Open back-stitching

Sellotape is used in the make up of the finger-stalls.

String. A strong thin string is recommended for the insertion of the eyes and in leather piping.

Greaseproof paper and *carbon paper*, red if possible, for use in making the card templates.

Eyes. Glass or perspex eyes in pairs on wire. Other types are available but some require the use of special tools.

A multiple punch is a useful tool for cutting small round holes.

Pipe cleaners. Used as stiffeners to give extra support to legs, etc.

Whiskers. Not less than 12 inch lengths of real horsehair are best for this purpose rather than man-made fibres.

Adhesive. U.H.U. or similar clear adhesives.

Bifurcated paper clips for the make up of collars.

Bias binding. The thin mercerised type is best for binding the edges and for some seams on the garments.

Press studs. A large size to attach the back legs of some puppets, and small ones for fastening garments.

STITCHES

The advantages of hand sewing were stated in the section on Seams and Edges (see page 10), and the following are stitches used by hand to make the puppets in this book:

Back-stitching. This is recommended for firmly stitched inside seams on felt and on fur fabrics (Diagram 2).

Open back-stitching is used for the same purpose and is a variation of the above, but because a space is left between the stitches, it is quicker to work, while still as firm and secure as close back-stitching (Diagram 3). (It will be

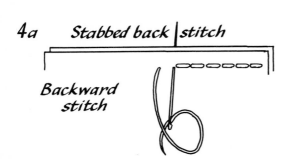

4a *Stabbed back | stitch*

Backward stitch

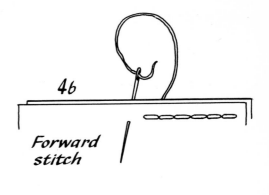

4b

Forward stitch

OVERSEWING

5

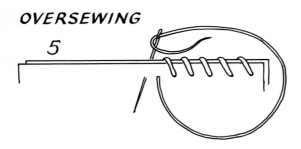

DOUBLE OVERSEWING

6a

Moving forward to next stitch

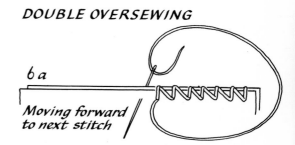

6b

Making second stitch in the same hole

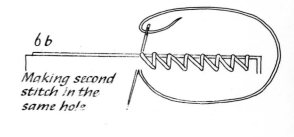

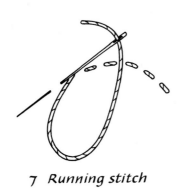

7 Running stitch

STAB STITCHING

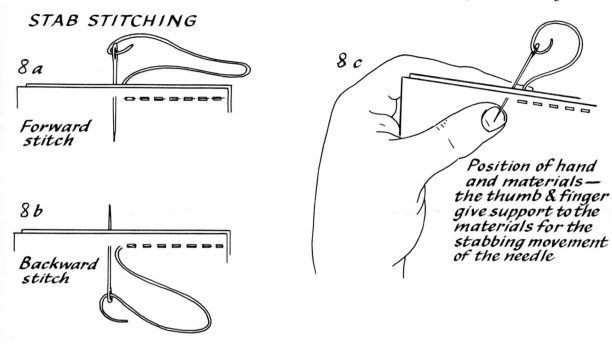

8 a

Forward stitch

8 b

Backward stitch

8 c

Position of hand and materials— the thumb & finger give support to the materials for the stabbing movement of the needle

open back-stitching which is referred to throughout this book unless the close back-stitching is specifically mentioned.)

Stabbed back-stitching. Where more than two thicknesses of material are to be sewn together on a seam a stabbed back-stitch is necessary to include all the materials. It is worked in two movements as shown in Diagrams 4a and 4b.

Oversewing. This is used to secure raw edges and is shown in Diagram 5.

Double oversewing is firmer than the above and is used on some of the short inside felt seams (see Diagrams 6a and 6b). The needle is passed through each hole twice making a diagonal and a vertical stitch. (This is sometimes referred to as the Streatley stitch and is used in gloving.)

Running stitches are needed for the insertion of gathering threads and for French seams and is shown in Diagram 7.

Stab-stitching. Holding the materials straight between finger and thumb, this is a running stitch worked in two movements for each stitch, as in Diagrams 8a, 8b and 8c. It is used for outside seams on felt, etc.

9. DETACHED CHAIN STITCHES

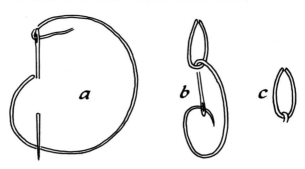

Chain-stitching. This is used singly in the making up of beaks and noses. See Diagram 9a, 9b and 9c.

Hemming is needed on the cotton garments, etc. Hems can be stitched up with hemming or slip-stitched as in dressmaking, showing very little on the outside (Diagram 10).

Tacking. Large running stitches which are used to secure two or more materials together before sewing the seams, etc.

Invisible tacking is used to keep fur fabric turnings in place such as round the neck edges, etc., when the folded edge is afterwards sewn to another part with ladder-stitching. To make the tacking invisible from the outside, self-coloured cotton is used and, while the usual large stitches are worked on the inside, very small stitches are made on the right side in the pile of the fabric, where they will not show and can be left in permanently.

Coloured tacking. This is used when it is necessary to repeat or transfer the inside marking out lines, such as position lines, on to the outside of the

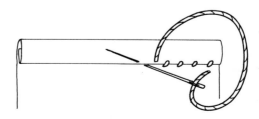

10 Hemming

11 a LADDER STITCH

*Tighten the thread while the stitching progresses to close the seam as at **a***

11 b
1. *The result of one row of ladder stitching on felt*

2. *The result after a second row has been worked along the same seam*

material. The tacking, in a contrasting colour, can be sewn in large stitches and removed later if necessary.

Invisible stitching. It is frequently stated in the instructions that the stitching is to be worked invisibly, especially in joining two pieces of felt which have been stuck together. This is to ensure that the two surfaces remain attached. The stitching is executed in the thickness only of the felts as for the Clown's features, etc., and should not show on the outside.

Ladder-stitching (Diagrams 11a and 11b). This important form of stitching will be required on all the puppets. As will be seen in Diagram 11a the name describes the ladder like position of the stitches before the thread is drawn up. It is used where an inside seam is worked from the outside when it would not be possible to do otherwise. It is also invaluable to attach ears, legs, etc., so that the stitching is invisible and strong. Diagram 11b shows one row of stitching joining two folded edges of material forming a seam. Be sure that the needle is inserted exactly opposite to where it came out of the previous stitch. A second row of ladder-stitching is necessary to complete the line of stitching which is worked by picking up the material on the needle which was a space between two stitches in the first row. With two rows of stitching a straighter line will result than with one row as well as being much stronger. (Compare Diagrams 11b, 1 and 2.)

Gathering. This is a form of stitching which holds fullness in one piece of fabric which is to be attached to a flat edge. This is used to help produce a good modelled effect on heads. Some pattern pieces, in the flat, are shaped by reducing the length or part of some edges by using gathers to draw up the material. The small running stitches used for the gathers are worked on the

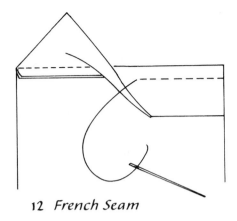

12 French Seam

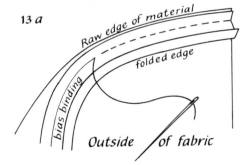

13 a

Attaching bias binding to raw edges
of fabric. (1st. row of stitching)

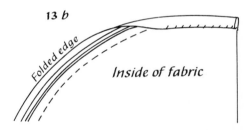

13 b

2nd. row. Binding folded over on
to the inside and hemmed in
position allowing the binding to
show equally on both sides of
the fabric edge

13 c

Bias binding

Inside of fabric

Binding showing on the
inside only having been
pulled fully over the first
seam after first row of
stitching in 12 a

outside of the marking out line on fur fabrics and as near the edge as possible on felt. Groups of gathers are also used to create wrinkles on the faces of some puppets.

French seam (Diagram 12). This is suitable for lightweight or cotton materials. First place the wrong sides together, and with running stitches, sew along the $\frac{1}{4}$ inch turning at $\frac{1}{8}$ inch from the edge. Reverse the seams placing the right sides of the material together and stitch the second line of running at $\frac{1}{8}$ inch from the folded edge of the first line of stitching, which will then be enclosed by the second row.

To attach bias binding. A thin mercerised bias binding will be needed to protect the raw edges of turnings on various puppets and as a trimming on the edges of some garments where it can be in a contrasting colour as a decorative finish. To reduce the width of bindings to keep them more in proportion with the small articles required for puppets, it is suggested that one turning is cut off and the edge turned in again. Treated in this way the binding is suitable to use on turnings of less than $\frac{1}{4}$ inch or on raw edges as a trimming. Following Diagrams 13a, 13b and 13c to attach the bias binding, place it to the raw edge of the material as at 13a, and attach it with running or back-stitching. Pass the binding over the edge of the material (Diagram 13b), fold up the second turning and hem in place along the stitching of the first row.

OTHER PROCESSES

The application of Iron-on Vilene

To reinforce or give support to some materials Iron-on Vilene can be satisfactorily applied. Place the rough side of this kind of Vilene to the back of the material and press it on with a fairly warm iron. It is not necessary to include it in the turnings on felt or fur fabrics, so that the pattern pieces requiring Vilene can be marked and cut out slightly smaller than the templates. Next place, pin and iron it to the back of the pieces of fabric concerned.

Insertion of whiskers

Lengths of horsehair are more suitable than man-made fibres for the whiskers of puppets. Thread about 12 inches of hair into a long darning needle and

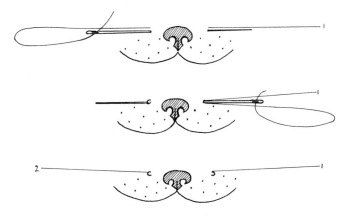

14   *Insertion of whiskers*

use the rows of dots on the pattern for the position of the whiskers. Diagram 14 shows the passage of the needle to and fro through the nose to secure each pair of whiskers. Check that each whisker cannot be pulled out. Add one more passage through the nose if required. Trim the whiskers and curve them if necessary to make an orderly group, alike on each side of the face.

The use of bifurcated paper clips
These can be used for attaching small buckles to plastic or leather collars and also as decoration on collars if required. Bifurcated clips used as shown in Diagram 15 will secure a small buckle to a plastic or leather collar end. Additional ones along the collar form a suitable decoration. On the back of the collar the tips should be turned back on themselves to shorten the length and as a safeguard against damage from the pointed ends.

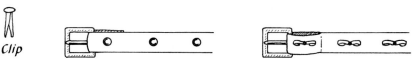

Clip

15   *Use of bi-furcated paper clips to make collars*

The use of large press studs (see Fox Terrier Diagrams 12h and 12j)

If the back legs of the Cat, and Dog and Pig puppets are required as detachable limbs, they can be affixed by using very large press studs (at least ½ inch). Place the fastening in the centre of the inner side of each back leg and the corresponding half at the side of the base of the glove. The least obtrusive half of the press stud is best on the glove, covered by a circle of thin felt with a small centre hole, allowing the other half of the stud to operate through it (Diagram 12h). The edge of the stud on the leg can be covered by a ring of thin felt (Diagram 12j). Attach each piece of felt by finely hemming round the outside edge.

EYES AND METHODS OF INSERTION

The bright natural colouring of glass or perspex eyes, obtainable in pairs on a wire, are very suitable for puppets. Sometimes they are mounted on a circle of felt or leather cut slightly larger than the eyes making an effective edging. Some eyes are improved with the addition of eyelids as used for Pigaletto.

Three methods are given for the puppets in this book.

Method I (for the Hen and Duck)

This is one of the simplest ways of preparing glass or perspex eyes and is suitable for the side facing eyes of poultry (Diagram 16a). They are attached to the 'side of head' pieces of felt before the head seams are closed.

For each eye:
a. Pierce with a thick needle the centre of a small piece of pale yellow felt (slightly larger than the eye).
b. Cut the wire joining the pair of eyes, 2 inches behind each. Pass each wire through the hole in the felt.
c. With a very small amount of adhesive placed in the centre back of the eye, stick the felt to the eye.
d. Cut the felt round the eye allowing just sufficient to show beyond it for an effective edging.

EYES   *Method I*

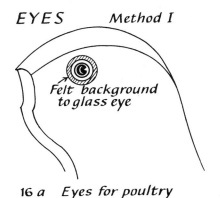

16 *a*   **Eyes for poultry**
Side facing position

16 *b*

Wire bent flat after
being inserted through the circle
of felt attached to the inside of
the head

16 *c*

Wire coiled round flat on the
circle of felt inside the head

e. Pierce the eye position on the head felt with the thick needle and pass the wire through to the back of the felt.

f. Cut a 1 inch circle of felt, pierce a centre hole and thread it on to the wire on the inside of the head.

g. Stick this circle to the inside of the head and then press the wire gently over to lie flat on the back of it (Diagram 16b).

h. Coil the wire round flat on the felt circle as in Diagram 16c, and then stitch the wire to the felt circle, also shown in the diagram.

Method II (eyes with a circle as background suitable for the Siamese Cat and the Teddy family)

For each eye:

a. Cut the wire leaving $1\frac{1}{4}$ inches behind each eye (Diagram 17a).

b. Take a small piece of felt or leather, slightly larger than the eye and of the colour suggested in the instructions for the puppets. With a thick needle pierce a hole in the centre.

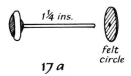

1¼ ins.

felt
circle

17 *a*

17 *b* Wire coiled
into a double shank

c. Put a little adhesive on the back of the eye and pass the wire through the hole in the felt, sticking the felt to the eye. With curved scissors trim the felt to form a narrow ring round the eye.

d. With a pair of round nosed pliers, coil up the wire into a double shank ending close to the eye as shown in Diagram 17b.

The eye is now ready to be inserted when the head has been stuffed.

Method III (eyes with lids suitable for the Pigs)

Prepare each eye as follows:

a. Cut the wire $1\frac{1}{4}$ inches behind each eye and cut out the flesh pink oval felt eye piece as shown in Diagram 18a.

b. Pierce a hole in the felt with a thick needle in the position shown in the diagram and pass the wire through it. With a small drop of adhesive on the back of the eye stick the felt to it.

c. The top part of the oval is brought forward and stuck to the front of the eye (Diagram 18b).

d. Cut away any surplus felt round the lower part of the eye leaving only a narrow edging.

e. The corners of the lid can be shaped and positioned with a few small stitches.

f. With round-nosed pliers, coil up the wire into a double shank as in Diagram 17b.

The eyes are now ready to be inserted when the head is stuffed.

EYES Method III (with eyelids)

18a Comparative size of felt oval to use as an eyelid and position of hole for the wire

18b Felt oval folded over top part of eye

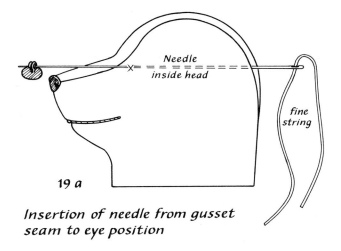

19 a

Insertion of needle from gusset seam to eye position

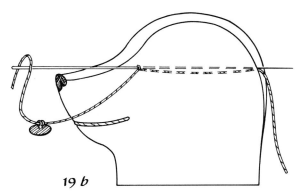

19 b

Return of needle to gusset seam with eye on string

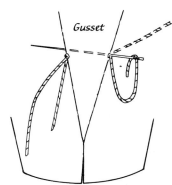

19 c **Back of Head**
The ending off of the strings

The insertion of eyes for Method II and III

Before making up the heads the exact place for each eye should be taken from the eye position given on the pattern and marked by a coloured tacking taken through to the front from the pencil spot on the back of the material.

Temporarily place a pair of hat pins in these positions and check that they are level and in the best place to get a good expression. (Reference should be made to the photographs of the puppets concerned.) Remove the hat pins after checking and clearly mark the holes. At this spot snip a tiny cross with the hole in the centre. It should be just large enough to enable the shank to be drawn back under the material, leaving the eye to rest on the surface of the fabric.

In Method II for the Dog, Cat and Teddies, the eyes should face forwards near the level of the 'stop' between the front of the head and the nose.

Insert and attach each eye as follows:

a. Thread a double long darning needle with a 12 inch length of strong thin string. Follow Diagram 19a and insert it between the stitching in the gusset seam and through the head, avoiding the finger-stall to come out at the small cross cut in the eye position, leaving the end of the string hanging at the back.

b. Place the prepared eye on the needle and string as shown in Diagram 19b. Insert the needle through the same position exactly and return in close proximity to the first string to the same spot in the gusset seam. Pull the eyes well back into the head with the shank under the fabric as explained above.

c. Tie the two ends together with a reef knot making the knot disappear inside the seam. Thread one end of the string into the needle and pass it back through the hole to a point away from the knot where it is brought out, and cut off on the surface of the material. Treat the second end in the same way in the opposite direction (Diagram 19c).

The eyes for Method III for the Pigs are inserted in the same way as in Method II, but the strings are crossed to the opposite sides at the back of the head as shown in Diagram 20. This will place the eyes diagonally between a front and side position which is suitable for the Pigs.

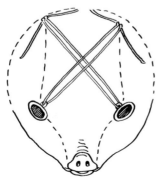

20 Eyes placed diagonally as for Pigs etc. Each string tied at ear positions

PATTERNS

How to make the templates

The patterns given are the actual sizes needed for the puppets in this book. As well as the full size patterns, half sizes for smaller hands have been included for several of the designs. Any other size can be made by reducing the pattern pieces as required, for which methods are fully described in the author's book *The Craft of Stuffed Toys*.

It is essential to use card templates for marking out, and thin sheets of coloured or white card are obtainable. To transfer the patterns on to the card, place a piece of greaseproof paper over the pattern page required and pencil along the outlines of the various pattern pieces. Insert all letters and marks of instruction given on each piece and be sure that the shapes are accurately drawn. The outlines are then transferred to the card by use of a carbon paper (red, if available to avoid smudginess). Place the carbon on the card under the greaseproof paper and keep all in place with paper clips or bulldog clips. Draw lightly but accurately over the pattern lines, letters and instructions. Remove the clips, carbon and tracing. Because it is easier to handle small pieces of card, cut roughly round each card template about $\frac{1}{8}$ inch outside the edge and then cut each single piece accurately to the actual pattern edge. Check the shape, size and information on the templates with each piece given on the pattern pages. Make quite sure that the small pattern pieces are correct as they so often increase in size. Pierce the dotted position lines with a thick needle to spot through them with a pencil point when marking out.

If any difficulty is experienced in using a pattern which has to be used for a *pair* of pieces, it can be cut out twice and the instructions put on the reverse side of *one* template. Card templates can be threaded on to a piece of string to prevent loss when not in use.

Garment patterns for the puppets

The patterns for garments which are best pinned to the materials as in Dressmaking should be made in thin paper, so the greaseproof tracing can be cut out and used instead of making it into card templates.

HOW TO USE THE PATTERN TEMPLATES

Marking out

First study the instructions given for the pattern. The materials should be smooth and laid flat on a firm surface with the back or inside upwards. When using fur fabrics note the direction in which the pile strokes and mark it with an arrow on the back of the material. Place out the templates as shown on each chart applicable to the material and colours being used. Allow space for the turnings if required. Check which pieces have to be reversed, if a pair of pieces are needed.

To mark out round the template edges, a well sharpened pencil or tailor's chalk should be used. Heavy marking out lines are not required, only just sufficient pressure is needed to show a light line for cutting out and as a stitch line on fur fabrics. A dark marking pencil used lightly will not drag the material out of place under the templates. Use pencil or chalk in a vertical position. The marking out can be done either by spotting or a continuous line drawn as close to the edges of the templates as possible, but great accuracy is needed all the time and firm pressure should be kept on each template to keep it in position.

Cutting out

Accuracy is essential. Use a sharp-pointed pair of scissors of comfortable size for the main parts. The under blade should rest on a firm surface or on a finger of the hand holding the material, to steady the work.

It is advisable first to cut out roughly beyond the edge of each pattern piece on the material, and then to make the final cut round each single piece, as it is easier to cut out accurately on a smaller amount of fabric.

Felt is usually cut out without turnings so smooth exact cuts are required, using as much of the blade as possible to avoid notching the edge of the felt. The marking out line should be left just on the waste material, Diagram 21a. A light pull on the felt will help to get a smooth continuous line round large curves. Very small pieces of felt or leather can be cut out by firmly holding the template on the material between a finger and thumb, and closely cutting round it. Always check that small pieces are not larger than the templates.

The cutting out on fur fabrics needs as much care as on felt. To allow for

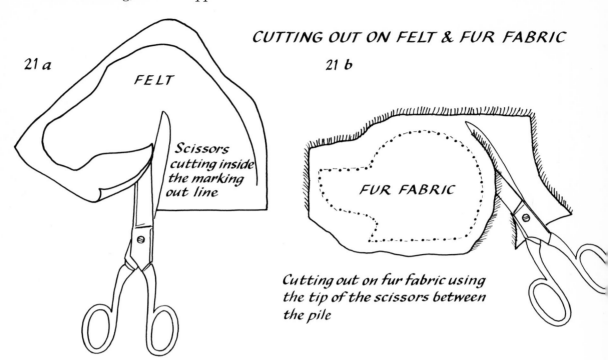

CUTTING OUT ON FELT & FUR FABRIC

21 a

FELT

Scissors cutting inside the marking out line

21 b

FUR FABRIC

Cutting out on fur fabric using the tip of the scissors between the pile

the turnings for this fabric the cutting out should be $\frac{1}{4}$ inch outside the marking out line. To avoid cutting away the pile, push the tip of the scissor blade between the pile before cutting and only make short cuts at a time (Diagram 21b).

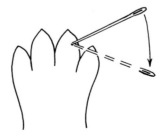

22   *The use of a strong needle to gently ease filling into pointed sections or small parts*

FILLINGS AND HOW TO USE THEM

The three fillings which can be used for stuffing the heads and other parts of the puppets are:

1. Rayon, Terylene or similar soft artificial filling which is clean, light in weight, easy to use and washable.
2. 'Foam' chippings, the familiar multi-coloured chips used for cushions or in upholstery, mixed with rayon makes good soft filling.
3. Woodwool—a shredded wood product used for packing china and other goods. Available free from shopkeepers. Use only clean material and free from dust. Woodwool of a medium stiffness is best to mix with the soft fillings, and is firmer than a soft filling mixed with foam chippings, for some of the puppets.

Either of the last two materials should be mixed evenly with the soft filling and made into 'cushions' of stuffing in sizes and shape suitable to occupy the various positions in a head, e.g. the top of the head, the nose and sides of the face, etc. Use the second filling (No. 2 or 3) as the centre of each 'cushion' and add more soft filling round the outside. Place them into the rounded or shaped parts of the head and fill the centre with a slightly firmer filling.

Small amounts of soft filling can be added where required to fill any cavities and to give additional modelling to the head, using a wedge shaped stuffing stick (Diagram 1, page 12).

A strong needle can be used to gently lever very small amounts of filling into small sections or pointed parts of paws, etc., as shown in Diagram 22.

Intelligent use of these cushions can improve and support the shapes which the pattern design intends the puppet to have. So insert the cushions into the head in a way that helps the contours and does not distort the shape.

Avoid over-stuffing the base of the head round the finger-stall which would reduce its capacity to contain the finger for the manipulation of the puppet.

THE 'GLOVE'

Several puppets in this book are so designed that their garments can be used as the hand covering instead of the 'glove' style, e.g. the Bears. This adds contrast and gives opportunity to introduce bright clothing with the natural animal colours. Additionally there is the added interest in a variety of garments for use.

The patterns and instructions for the foundation garments used as the hand covering are given with the puppets requiring them. The plain glove for the Dogs, Cats and Pigs is made from the pattern on page 32 and the small size puppet from the pattern on page 33. With this plain 'glove' the hand manipulating the puppet can be inserted at the base of the glove or through a slit across the centre back (see pattern). Should the position of the slit be unsuitable it can be placed a little higher or lower as desired. With the optional addition of back legs to this plain glove style, the slit across the back is recommended.

The make-up of the glove parts and the insertion of the 'arm' or sleeve and head for Pigaletto, the Fox Terrier and the Siamese Cat.

   a. Place the back and front parts of the glove, right sides together. Pin and back-stitch the two side seams.

   b. Turn up the hem along the fold line and neatly sew it in place without showing stitches on the outside. Do not close the shoulder seams at this stage in the work.

   c. The sleeves. To accommodate the upward position of the thumb and fingers while using puppets, the sleeves are inserted in an inverted position and each sleeve seam and shoulder seam are stitched as one seam from the wrist to the neck. Working with the sleeve right side out and the glove inside out, place the sleeve into the armhole as in Diagram 22a, front edge to front edge as marked on the pattern. Pin and back-stitch the armhole seam starting and ending at the shoulder.

   d. Turn the sleeve inside out and starting at the wrist (Diagram 22b), back stitch the sleeve seam to the shoulder and then continue to the neck, closing the shoulder seam.

(Continued on page 37)

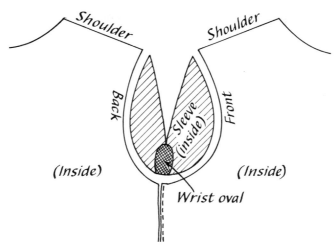

22 a Insertion of sleeve when the sleeve seam and shoulder
seam are worked as one continuous seam, starting at
the wrist oval. Pin sleeve to armhole in this position
and stitch armhole seam

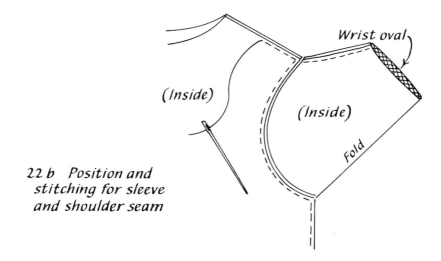

22 b Position and
stitching for sleeve
and shoulder seam

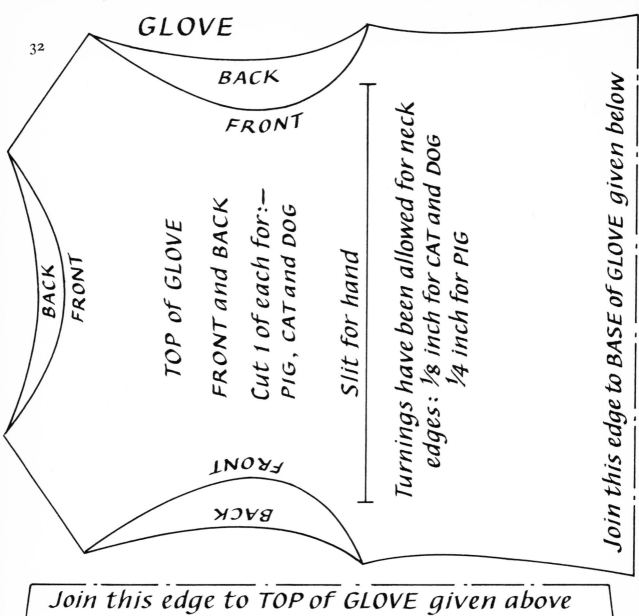

32

GLOVE

BACK

FRONT

BACK
FRONT

TOP of GLOVE

FRONT and BACK

Cut 1 of each for:—
PIG, CAT and DOG

Slit for hand

Turnings have been allowed for neck
edges: ⅛ inch for CAT and DOG
¼ inch for PIG

FRONT

BACK

Join this edge to BASE of GLOVE given below

Join this edge to TOP of GLOVE given above

BASE of GLOVE

Cut 1 for front
Cut 1 for back

Allow ½ inch turnings for HEM

GLOVE for SMALL PUPPETS

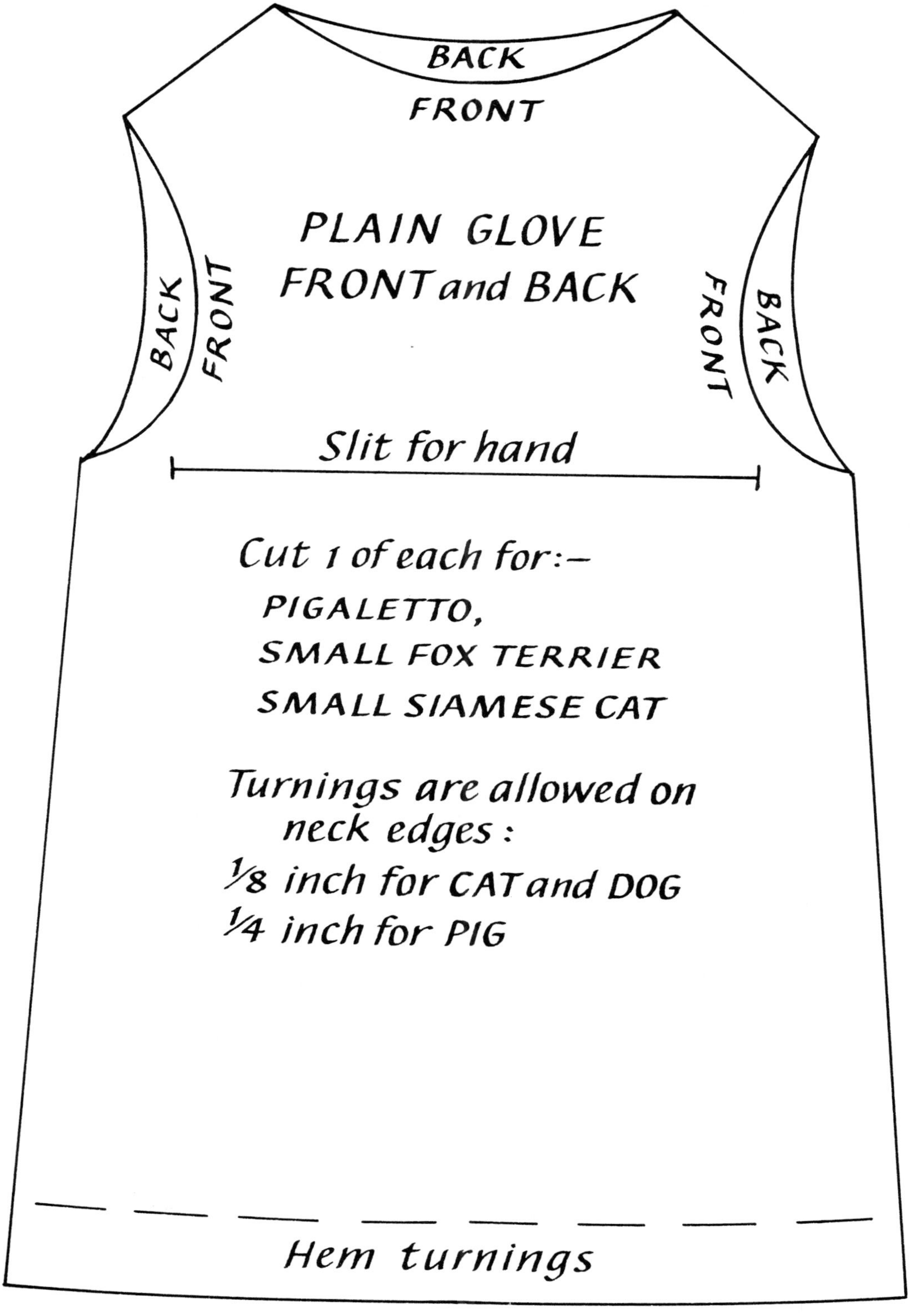

BACK

FRONT

BACK FRONT

FRONT BACK

PLAIN GLOVE FRONT and BACK

Slit for hand

Cut 1 of each for:—

PIGALETTO,

SMALL FOX TERRIER

SMALL SIAMESE CAT

Turnings are allowed on neck edges:

1/8 inch for CAT and DOG

1/4 inch for PIG

Hem turnings

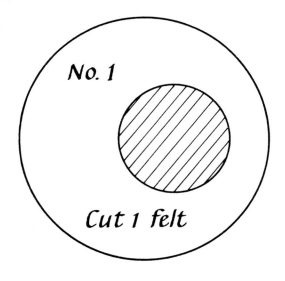

No. 1

Cut 1 felt

No. 1 CLOWN

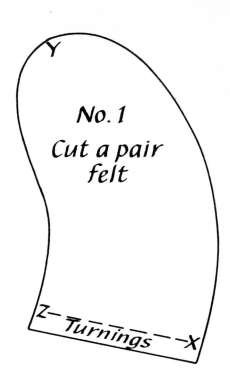

No. 1
Cut a pair
felt

Y

Z — Turnings — X

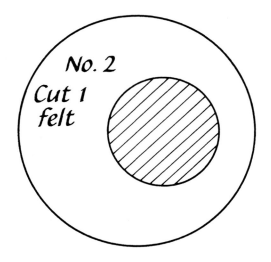

No. 2
Cut 1
felt

No. 2 HEN

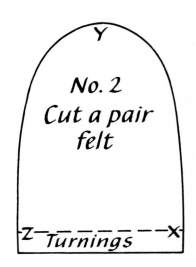

Y

No. 2
Cut a pair
felt

Z — Turnings — X

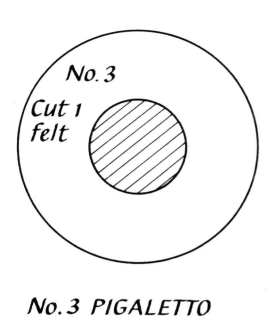

No. 3

Cut 1 felt

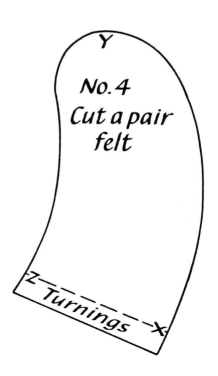

No. 3

Cut a pair felt

Y

Z — — — Turnings — — — X

No. 3 PIGALETTO

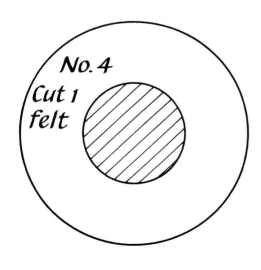

No. 4

Cut 1 felt

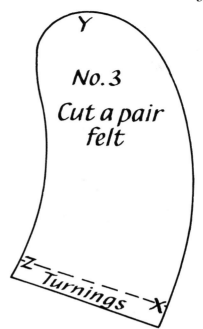

Y

No. 4

Cut a pair felt

Z — — — Turnings — — — X

No. 4 FOX TERRIER
SIAMESE CAT

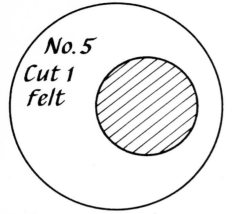

No. 5
Cut 1
felt

No. 5 and 6
Cut a pair
felt

Y

Z — Turnings — X

No. 5 DUCK and Mr. BEAR

No. 5 and No. 6

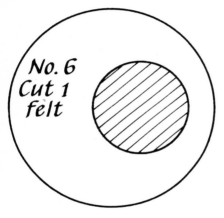

No. 6
Cut 1
felt

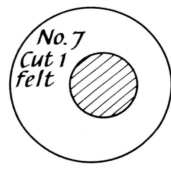

No. 7
Cut 1
felt

No. 7 or
No. 8
Cut a pair
felt

Y

Z Turnings X

No. 6 Mrs. BEAR

**No. 7 BETTY and BERNIE BEARS
SMALL FOX TERRIER
SMALL SIAMESE CAT**

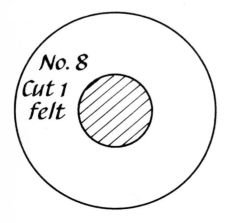

No. 8
Cut 1
felt

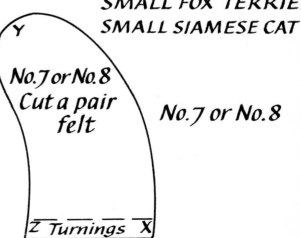

Y

No. 7 or No. 8
Cut a pair
felt

No. 7 or No. 8

Z Turnings X

No. 8 SMALL PIGALETTO

e. Turn the glove right side out and fold in a narrow turning round the neck edge and tack it in place.

f. To insert the head into the neck, place the folded neck edge over the stitch line round the felt circle on the base of the head, and pin evenly at the centre front and centre back and then at the shoulder seams. Add more pins as necessary and ladder-stitch the folded neck edge to the head, with two rows of stitching.

g. If the slit across the back is required, an $\frac{1}{8}$ inch of the edges should be turned in and invisibly hemmed down. Closely oversew round the ends of the slit to prevent the felt stretching.

THE FINGER-STALLS

A variety of sizes and shapes are given but those suggested are the best perhaps for the puppets concerned. For instance, the short, straight finger-stall is suitable for poultry, as this allows the heads to bend down to ground level. The curved finger stalls are more suited for heads of other types, especially the larger heads, as well as being more comfortable for some users. The position of the hole in the felt circle can be either in the centre of the circle or off centre. When it is off centre the hole is placed towards the back of the head. This also allows for greater forward movement. If changes are made in the selection of finger-stalls, the choice should be for one which gives the greatest comfort and ease of manipulation. It should also be noted that the base measurement is correct for the hole in the felt circle, the base of the finger-stall being slightly larger to allow for the two small seams. If the size of a puppet's neck becomes enlarged, for instance by the stretching of the fabric through over-stuffing, the size of the felt circle can be increased.

The make-up of the finger-stalls (Diagrams 23a–23e)
The following instructions apply to the curved or straight finger-stall.

a. Place the two felt finger-stall pieces together and back-stitch round the edge X-Y-Z. Leave the base open, X-Z (Diagram 23a).

b. A thin card ring as a stiffener is required to encircle the base of the stall. Cut a strip of thin card, $\frac{3}{8}$ inch wide ($\frac{1}{4}$ inch for the small size stall) and approximately 4 inches long which will curve round without cracking. The card cylinder in the centre of a toilet roll is usually ideal for this purpose as it is already curved and can be cut to the width and the length needed (Diagram 23b).

c. Leave the finger-stall unturned with the seam outside, and put it on a first finger. Place the card round the outside of it, $\frac{1}{4}$ inch above the base edge. Overlap the ends of the card so that it fits snugly but not too tightly (Diagram 23c). Hold it in place and wrap a narrow Sellotape across the joins, and then apply the Sellotape twice round the outside of the card ring—this gives additional strength for the stitching which follows.

d. Take the ring off the stall and take the stall from the finger. Put Sello-tape across the join on the inside of the ring. Replace the card ring on

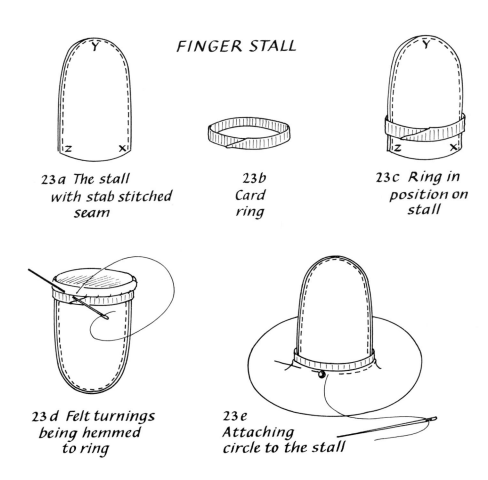

FINGER STALL

23a The stall
with stab stitched
seam

23b
Card
ring

23c Ring in
position on
stall

23d Felt turnings
being hemmed
to ring

23e
Attaching
circle to the stall

the stall, $\frac{1}{4}$ inch above its base, and fold the $\frac{1}{4}$ inch felt turnings up over it and pin in place. Hem the edge of the felt turning to the ring through the Sellotape and into the card using a fine strong thread and $\frac{1}{4}$ inch stitches (Diagram 23d). Next work a second row of hemming round the felt edge between the stitches of the first row. Place the felt circle for the base of the finger-stall over the top of the stall and slide it down to the base. The edge of the centre hole in the circle should now lie, facing upwards, just below the hemming on the turnings. Pin in position as shown in Diagram 23e and back-stitch $\frac{1}{16}$ inch from the edge into the turnings underneath, to secure the circle to the stall. It is now ready to be inserted into the head.

The insertion of the finger-stalls

This is done after the head is stuffed and light filling only has been placed in the neck. Also the $\frac{1}{4}$ inch turnings round the base of the head should have been folded and tacked in position. If the finger-stall hole is not in the centre of the felt circle it must be placed towards the back of the neck and a curved finger-stall should point towards the front (Diagram 24a).

a. With a finger inside the stall push it up and through the neck into its position in the head until the felt circle at the base of the stall is level with the folded neck edge.

b. Remove the finger and temporarily fill the stall with soft filling until the stuffing round the neck is completed.

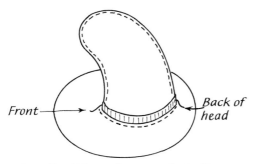

24 a *Position of curved stall when placed towards back of circle*

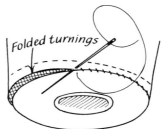

24 b *Attaching felt circle on finger stall to the base of the head*

c. Using a flat stuffing stick, add sufficient filling in small quantities to stuff the neck round the stall down to the circle. The circle should be kept as flat as possible.

d. Oversew the edge of the felt circle to the fold of the turnings round the neck. If necessary trim the edge of the felt (Diagram 24b).

e. Remove the filling in the stall.

EMBROIDERY STITCHES FOR GARMENTS

Running stitches, back-stitches or chain stitches to which is added whipping, lacing or threaded stitches in contrasting colours, form a useful and simple basis for decoration of very small garments.

Back-stitches and running stitches of approximately $\frac{1}{8}$ inch are suitable in size for the foundation stitches. Chain stitching can be the same or a little larger according to the thickness of the material and thread used.

Six stranded embroidery cottons or similar threads are suggested.

A blunt tapestry needle is helpful for the lacing and whipping under the threads of the foundation stitches.

Diagrams 25–28b illustrate a few ways suitable for small garments. Many other ideas can be obtained from books of embroidery stitches.

Embroidery Stitches as Decorative borders on small garments

a   b

25

Whipped running stitch. (a) with one colour thread. (b) Using two colours

a   b

26

Laced running   stitches—using one (a) or two (b) contrasting colours

a   b

27

Two rows running stitch threaded with one (a) or two (b) contrasting colours

28a
Chain stitch

28 b

Whipped chain stitch

Pigaletto and Family

This popular group of puppets is made up in flesh pink felt but other natural colourings could be used. Mr. Pigaletto has a butcher's apron and Mrs. Pigaletto a more feminine front. A small size pattern has been included for the junior members of the family who can be dressed with aprons or any other suitable garments such as those given for the Teddy Bears. All the family are made from the same instructions.

Materials required for the full size puppet:

12 in. × 30 in. flesh pink felt.
$4\frac{1}{2}$ in. × 7 in. white felt for collar.
20 inches of 1 inch wide ribbon (blue and white check or spotted ribbon) for bow tie.
1 pair of 9 mm. blue glass eyes.
A thread of dark coral pink Anchor soft or stranded cotton for mouth marks and nostrils.
12 in. × 8 in. of navy and white striped cotton for butcher's apron (stripes in 12 inch direction).
$\frac{3}{4}$ yard white tape, $\frac{1}{4}$ inch wide for apron ties.
A pipe cleaner for the tail.
A small piece of stiff card for the nose.
A colourless adhesive.
Rayon or similar soft filling and woodwool.

Materials for the small size puppet:

10 in. × 24 in. flesh pink felt.
$3\frac{1}{2}$ in. × $5\frac{1}{2}$ in. white felt, for collar.
18 inches of 1 inch wide ribbon for bow tie (check or spotted).
1 pair of 7 mm. blue glass eyes.
8 in. × 6 in. of navy and white striped cotton for butcher's apron (stripes in 8 inch direction).
Other items as for full size puppet given above.

(Continued on page 51)

PIGALETTO

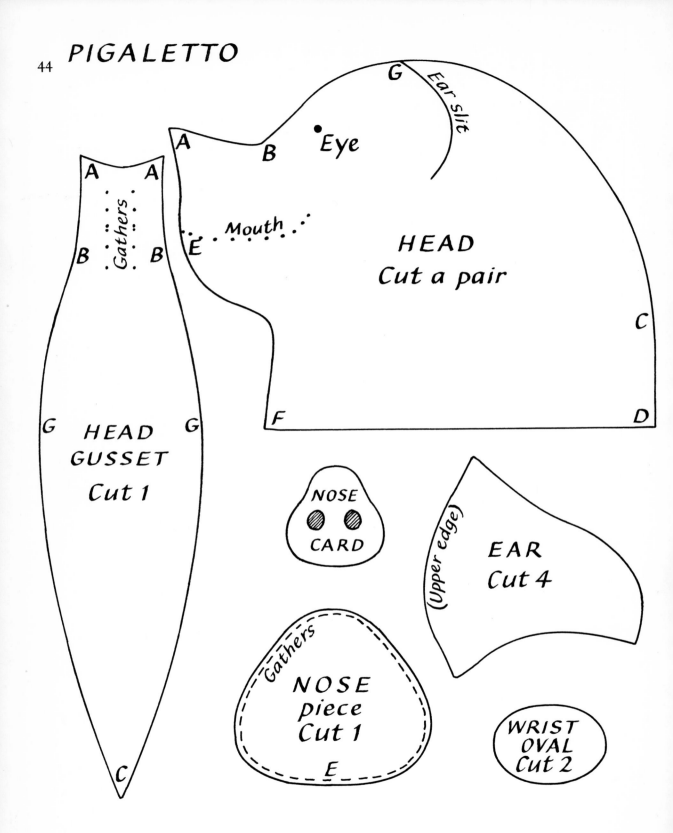

G

Ear slit

A B • Eye

A   A

Gathers

B   B   E ····· Mouth ···

HEAD
Cut a pair

G   HEAD   G
GUSSET
Cut 1

C

F   D

NOSE
○○
CARD

(Upper edge)

EAR
Cut 4

NOSE
piece
Cut 1

Gathers

E

WRIST
OVAL
Cut 2

C

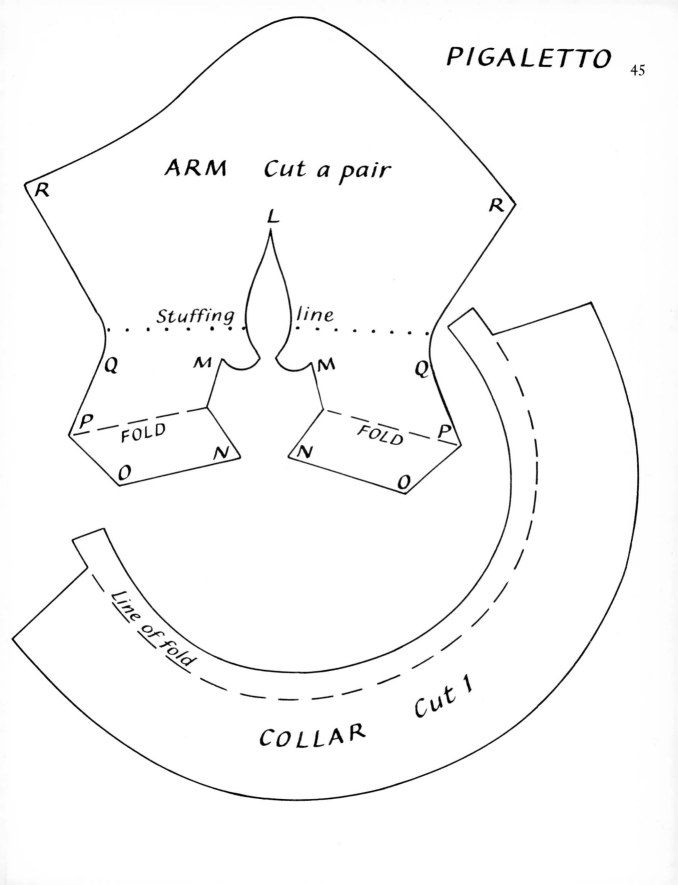

PIGALETTO 45

ARM   Cut a pair

Stuffing line

FOLD   FOLD

Line of fold

COLLAR   Cut 1

PIGALETTO

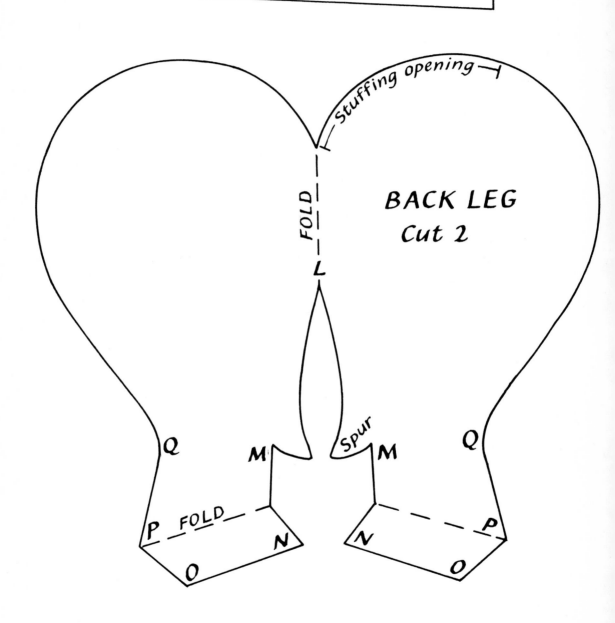

TAIL Cut 1 felt

FOLD

BACK LEG
Cut 2

Stuffing opening

FOLD

L

Spur

Q   M   M   Q

P   FOLD   N   N   P

O   O

PIGALETTO

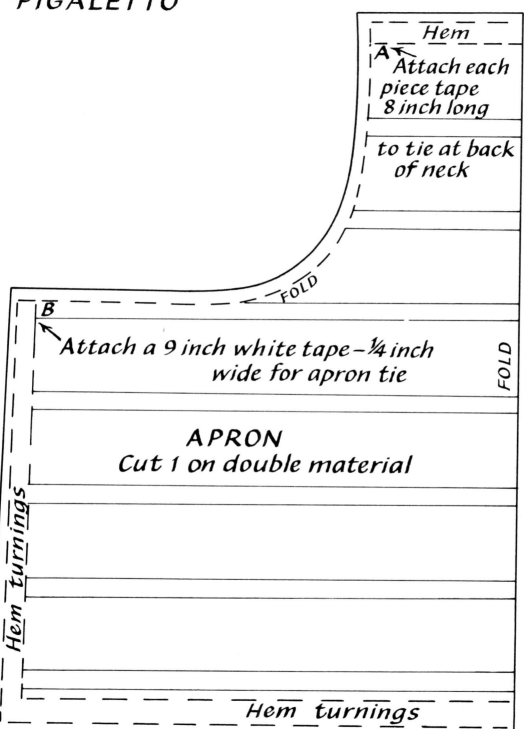

Hem

A Attach each piece tape 8 inch long

to tie at back of neck

FOLD

FOLD

B Attach a 9 inch white tape — ¼ inch wide for apron tie

APRON
Cut 1 on double material

Hem turnings

Hem turnings

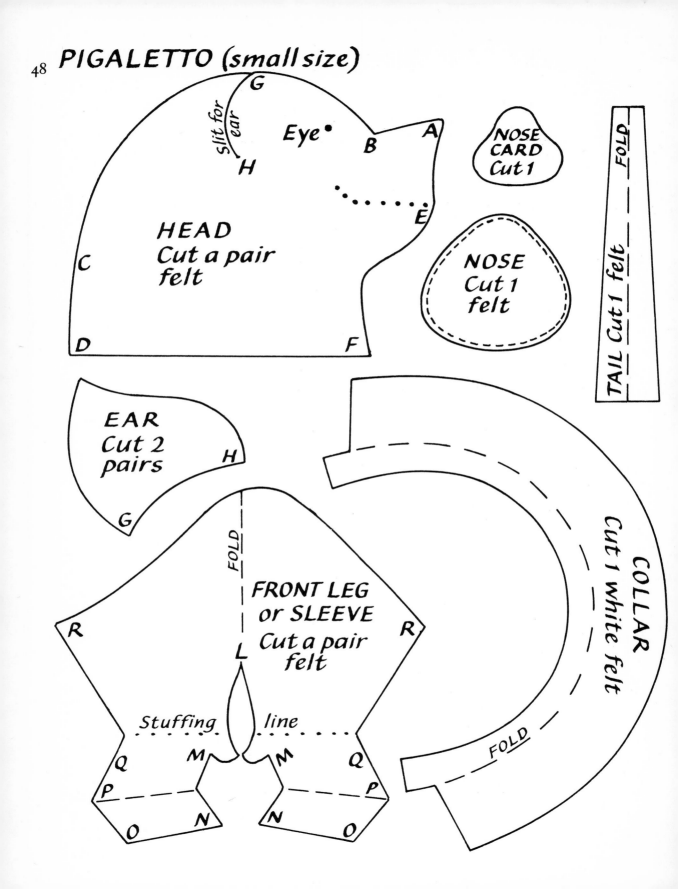

48 **PIGALETTO (small size)**

HEAD
Cut a pair
felt

G
slit for ear
Eye •
B
A
H
E
C
D
F

NOSE CARD
Cut 1

NOSE
Cut 1
felt

TAIL Cut 1 felt
FOLD

EAR
Cut 2
pairs
H
G

FRONT LEG
or SLEEVE
Cut a pair
felt

FOLD
L
R
R
Stuffing line
Q
M
M
Q
P
N
N
P
O
O

COLLAR
Cut 1 white felt
FOLD

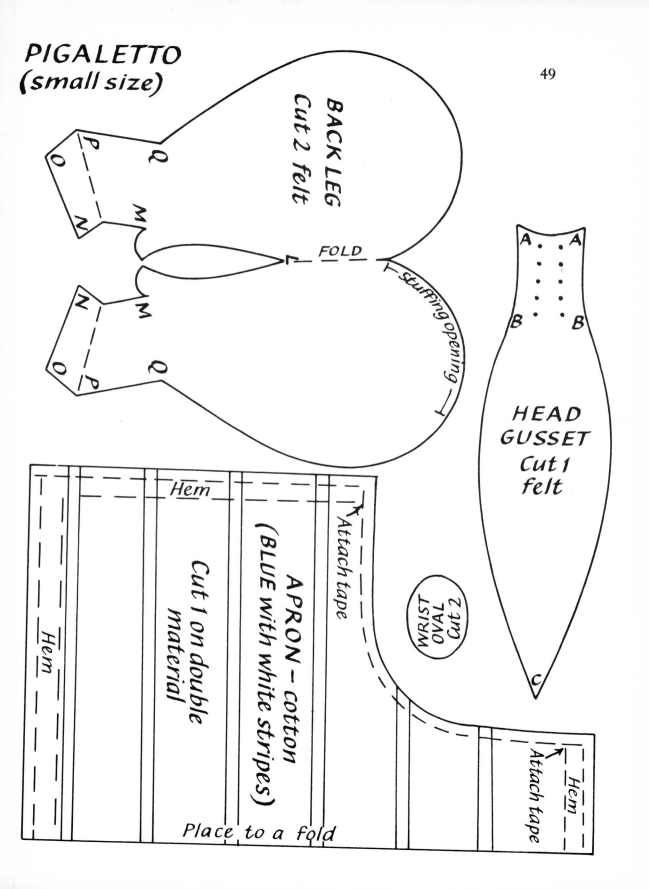

PIGALETTO
(small size)

49

BACK LEG
Cut 2 felt

O P Q
N M

FOLD

Stuffing opening

A · · A
· ·
· ·
· ·
B · · B

HEAD
GUSSET
Cut 1
felt

C

Hem

Attach tape

APRON—cotton
(BLUE with white stripes)

Cut 1 on double
material

WRIST
OVAL
Cut 2

Hem

Hem

Attach tape

Place to a fold

Pigaletto: Chart 1   Flesh pink felt   12″ × 30″

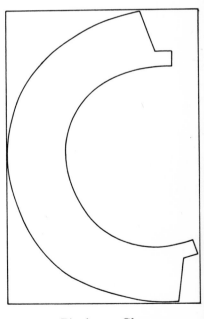

Pigaletto: Chart 2
White felt   4½″ × 7″

GENERAL INFORMATION

All seams are on the inside to get the smooth effect needed for this puppet and are open back-stitched. No turnings are required on the felt pieces unless stated on the pattern. References will be made to the instructions on technical points given on pages 9–41.

The card templates are made from the patterns on pages 44 to 47 (or 48 and 49 for small size) as instructed on page 26. Pierce the dotted position lines with a thick needle and arrange the pattern templates on the felt as shown on the charts on page 50.

Mark and cut out on the back of the felt as directed on page 27 with a very finely pointed pencil and cut out just inside the marking out lines. Pencil the dots through the holes along the position lines for the features, the gathers on the gusset and the stuffing lines on the front legs, and then sew in coloured tacking along the dotted lines to show well on the outside.

1 *Head showing ears with upper edge next to the gusset, also eyelid and nose*

1. *MAKE-UP OF THE HEAD*

The Ears. These are made and inserted into the head pieces before the head is made up.

    a. Two pieces of felt are used for each ear. Stick them together securely, spreading the adhesive thinly on one ear piece. This will stiffen the ears for the erect position required. Firmly press the edges of the ears together and trim off any adhesive after it has dried.

        To create the crinkly base of a pig's ear, make 5 or 6 long over-sewn stitches across the base and draw up the threads until the desired effect is obtained. End the thread securely. To attach the ears, cut the slits on the head pieces along the curved line for each ear position. Note that the upper edge of each ear should be placed to the top of the head, G to G (Diagram 1).

        Insert each ear into the slits from the outside to the inside of the head pieces. Place the base of the ears and the back edge of the slits level and evenly together, and oversew these three edges. Add the front edge of the slit and stab back-stitch all together.

    b. The Head pieces. The wrinkles on the nose end of the gusset are formed by two gathering threads. Pick up the spots on the needle without going right through the felt (Diagram 2a) and pull up the two threads to reduce the length to fit A B on the head (Diagram 2b).

    c. Pin one head piece to the head gusset at A B and C. Double oversew along the gathered section, A to B, then back-stitch the remainder of the seam to C. Repeat for the second head seam A B C and then continue to D.

    d. Pin and back-stitch the front seam E F.

    e. The Nose. This is made up with a padded card as follows: Cut the stiff card for the nose and punch the oval holes as shown in Diagram 3a. (Punch each hole twice, the second time slightly above the first to get the oval shape.) The card is padded to add thickness by wrapping it with long thin pieces of rayon filling, wound across and up and down the card, passing each side of the two holes to leave them clear (Diagram 3b). Keep it in place with cotton thread as shown in Diagram 3c, this time passing the cotton through the holes.

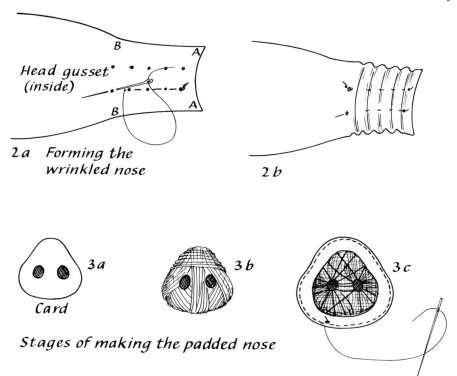

2a   Forming the
     wrinkled nose

2b

3a   Card

3b

3c

Stages of making the padded nose

Sew in the gathering thread round the edge of the felt nose piece, using small stitches, then place the wrapped card in the centre, at the back of the nose piece and pin in position. Draw up the edges of the felt over the padded card by pulling up the gathering thread a little as it is sewn in.

f. Using a thread of brown Anchor soft or similar embroidery cotton pass the needle through one nostril hole several times, forming satin stitches on the front. Pull each stitch tightly to take the felt back through the hole as far as possible and secure each stitch to the padding at the back. Repeat for the second nostril. This will form a realistic nose for a pig. Pull up the gathering thread tightly, drawing the felt well over the padded card and end securely.

g. Fold back $\frac{1}{8}$ inch of the felt edge as turnings round the hole formed for the nose and invisibly tack it in place. Turn the head right side out.

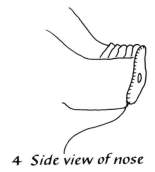

4 *Side view of nose*

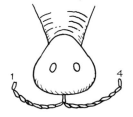

5 *Front view showing*
line of mouth

h. To attach the nose, place it in position, E to E, so that the folded edge lies between the gathering thread and the edge of the nose. This should allow the padded thickness round the edge of the nose to be on the outside of the head as in Diagram 4. Pin in position neatly. Ladder-stitch the nose to the folded felt edge, stitching round it twice.

i. Stuff the head with fairly firm cushions of rayon and a small amount of woodwool evenly mixed (see page 29). The nose should be filled first, then the crown, cheeks and finally the centre of the head. Stuff the neck lightly and complete the stuffing when the finger-stall is inserted.

2. THE FINGER-STALL

Make this from the pattern No. 3 on page 35. (Use No. 8 for the small size Pigaletto.) Make up and attach it as instructed on pages 37–40, completing the stuffing of the neck at the same time.

3. THE MOUTH MARKS (see Diagram 5)

These are worked over the tacking threads marking the position of the mouth. Using a dark salmon or similar shade of embroidery cotton, start with a knot at an eye position. Bring the needle out at 1 and work a long stitch from 1 to 4. Each end of the mouth should turn upwards a little to improve the expression. Make a small vertical stitch in the centre front (starting over the long stitch) to the base of the nose. End the thread in the second eye position where it will be covered by the eye.

4. THE EYES

Prepare and make up the lids as instructed on page 23 for Method III and as shown in Diagrams 18a and 18b (page 23). They are inserted at the tack marks. Check that the pair of eyes are level and even. (See page 25.)

5. THE FRONT LEGS OR 'ARMS'

Each leg is made up as follows:

a. Fold the leg exactly together and pin along the turnings, L M, then back-stitch this seam and from N–O (Diagram 6a).

b. To divide the front part of the hoof, fold it as in Diagram 6b and then back-stitch from P through Q/O to P and M/N to the folds. Close the seam Q R.

c. Turn the leg and well point the spur and the hooves with a flattened, blunt orange stick.

d. The two sections of the hooves are now stuffed lightly with rayon filling. Keep the centre division (seam O–N) pressed up in position between them (Diagram 6c). Stuff the spur and continue the filling to the stuffing line as indicated by the tacks.

e. Turn the leg down over the hoof to the level of the stuffing line (Diagram 6d) and attach the ovals of felt required to keep the stuffing in the hoof, invisibly hemming it to the inside of the leg felt along the stuffing line (Diagram 6e). Turn the top part of the leg right side out ready to insert it in the glove. To prevent the hooves from opening too much, ladder-stitch the inner sides together, $\frac{1}{4}$ inch above the base, sewing from the back to the centre only, to leave the front of the hooves open.

6. THE GLOVE

Follow the instructions on page 30 for the make-up of the glove, the insertion of the 'arms' and the attachment of the head to the glove.

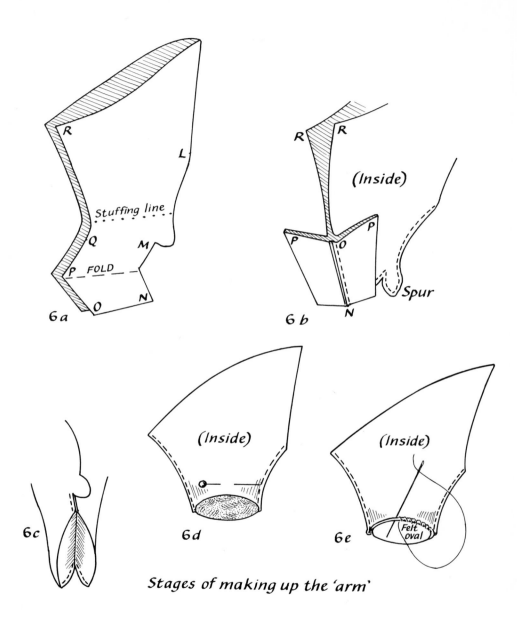

R

L

Stuffing line

Q   M

P   FOLD

O   N

6 a

R   R

(Inside)

P   P
        O

P

N

Spur

6 b

6 c

(Inside)

6 d

(Inside)

Felt
oval

6 e

Stages of making up the 'arm'

7. THE BACK LEGS (*optional*)

To make up each leg:

a. Fold the leg along the line indicated on the pattern and pin and back-stitch the seam L M and from N–O (Diagram 6a).

b. To divide the front part of the hoof, fold it as in Diagram 6b, then pin and back-stitch from P through Q/O to P and M/N to the folds.

c. Turn the hoof and spur right side out before continuing the inside seam to the stuffing opening.

d. Turn the whole leg right side out and point the hooves and spurs with a flattened, blunt orange stick.

e. Carefully stuff the hooves with soft filling and lever the stuffing into the points with a strong needle (see page 29, and Diagram 22). Turn the leg right side out and continue the stuffing to the opening. Close the stuffing opening with two rows of ladder-stitching (see page 17). Make the second leg and attach the legs to the base of the glove as shown in Diagram 7, with ladder stitching. If back legs are to be detachable they can be each secured by one large press stud (see page 21).

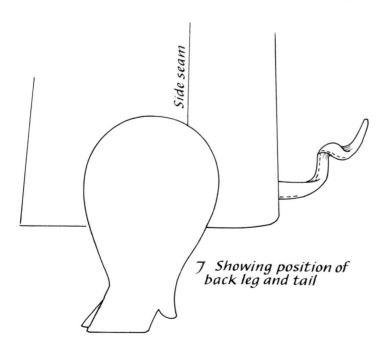

Side seam

7 *Showing position of back leg and tail*

8. THE TAIL

Place a pipe cleaner along the length of the felt tail piece. Fold the tail in half lengthways and starting at the tip, stab-stitch the tail seam near the edges of the felt, including the pipe cleaner as a core. As soon as the thickness of the pipe cleaner is not sufficient to fill the tail, bend it over and use it doubled. In addition, as the tail widens, lay in another narrower piece of felt under the pipe cleaner to fill the larger end of the tail and stab-stitch to the end of the seam. Attach the tail to the centre back of the glove at the hemline and stitch it in place securely. Curl the tail in the conventional porcine fashion, in an upwards direction (Diagram 7).

9. THE COLLAR AND BOW

Fold the collar as indicated on the pattern and attach it to the neck with a front fastening using a hook and eye or button and buttonhole. Place the ribbon round the neck under the turned down collar and tie it in the front with a tailored bow.

10. THE BUTCHER'S APRON

Use a navy, white striped cotton material with the stripes running across the apron.

a. Place and pin the half pattern to the folded material. Cut out along the edge of the pattern piece which includes the allowance for turnings as indicated.

b. Bind the curved seams from A to B by the method given on page 19 and shown in Diagram 13c on the same page. First cut the binding to a narrower width if desired by removing a turning.

c. Fold in the turnings for the top, sides and base, and hem them in place.

d. Attach the white $\frac{1}{4}$ inch tapes to tie the apron at the back at the waist and at the back of the neck. Sew the tapes to the inside of the apron.

11. MRS. PIGALETTO

This puppet is made from the same pattern as Mr. Pigaletto, but with a feminine apron instead of the butcher's apron. The felt collar should be made ¼ inch narrower than the pattern given and small buttons sewn on to the centre front of the glove will suggest a dress under the apron.

12. THE APRON (*decorated with embroidery*)

Material required:

$4\frac{1}{2}$ in. × $8\frac{1}{2}$ in. turquoise cotton.
Two 12 inch pieces of straight cotton tape for ties.

The top of the apron is gathered and set into a band. The base and sides can be hemmed or the edges turned up on the right side and covered with one of the decorative edgings, given in the diagrams on page 41. Rows of various whipped or laced running stitches, etc., can be worked to form a band of decoration above the hem.

Straight binding tape is used as apron strings and are attached as directed on the pattern.

The small Pig requires:

$3\frac{3}{4}$ in. × 7 in. cotton material.
Two 9 inch pieces straight binding tape.

Suki, the Siamese Cat

The well contrasted colours of a Siamese Cat makes it a pleasing choice for a glove puppet. The colours given here can be changed to suit any other variety of this breed.

A word of warning should be given however. This design aims at producing the distinctive features of a Siamese Cat. Any owner of a typical English domestic 'moggy' realises at once that there are differences. Do not, therefore, depart from the Siamese colourings and attempt to produce an English pussem, using this design. Perhaps of all animals the cat family have the most difficult characteristics to catch convincingly and especially in felt—most likely due to the differences between their skeletal formation and their furry contours.

Patterns for the full size and a small puppet are given. The small size is made up from the instructions for the larger puppet as they are the same in all respects except size. The small puppet is especially suitable for young performers.

Materials needed for the full size puppet:

12 in. × 24 in. oyster coloured felt for the main parts.
11 in. × 7½ in. dark brown felt for ears, nose, paws, tail and chin.
9 in. × 5 in. light chocolate brown felt for the remaining brown sections.
1 pair blue glass or perspex cat's eyes, size 13 mm.
A small piece of shiny black gloving leather for nose and eyes.
Several 12 inch lengths or one long length of cream or white horse hair for whiskers.
U.H.U. or similar colourless adhesive.
A 10 inch length of plastic beading or leather, ½ in. wide for the collar.
Rayon or similar soft filling and woodwool for stuffing.

(*Continued on page 69*)

SIAMESE CAT

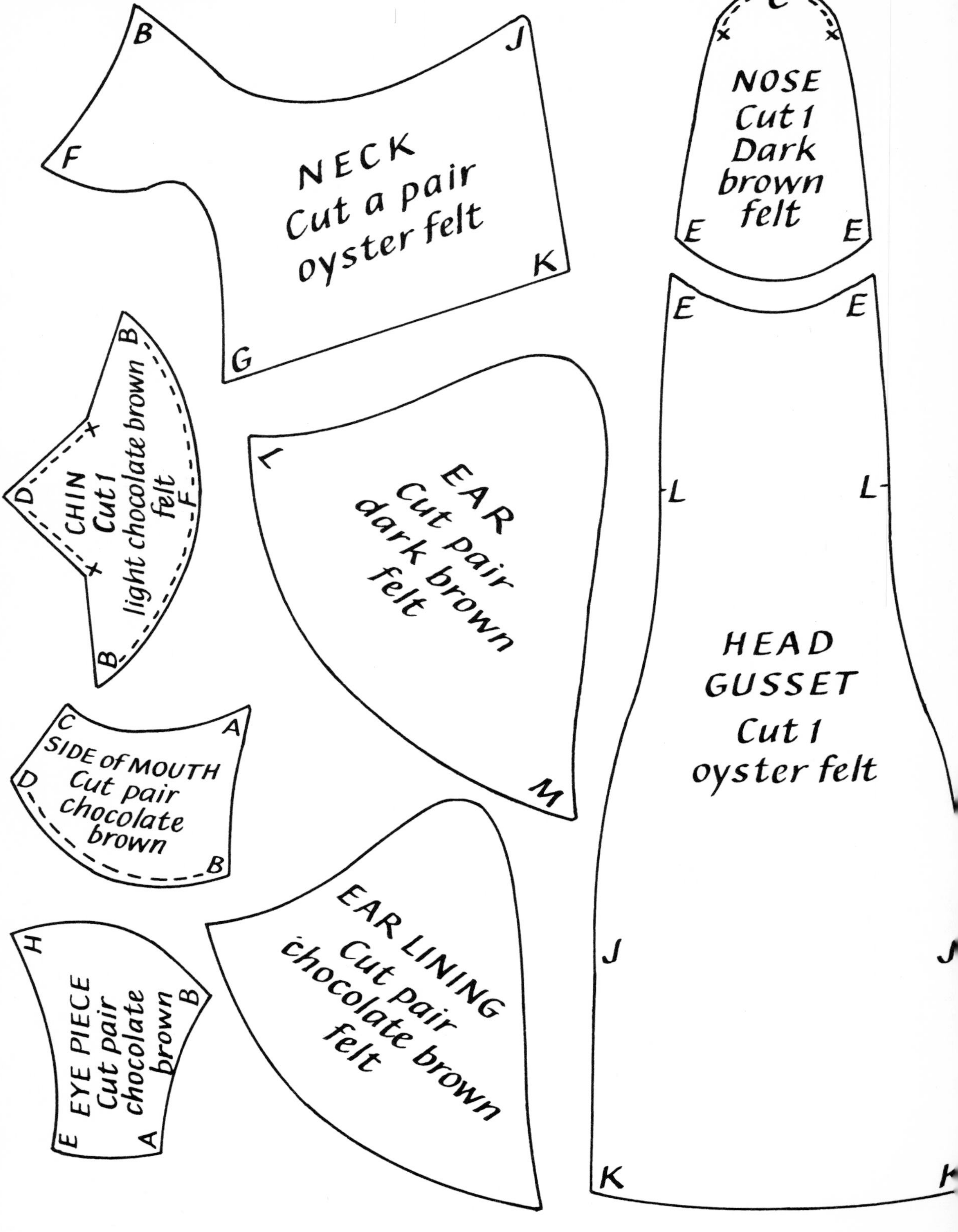

NECK
Cut a pair
oyster felt

(labels: B, J, F, K, G)

NOSE
Cut 1
Dark
brown
felt

(labels: C, E, E)

CHIN
Cut 1
light chocolate brown
felt

(labels: B, D, F, B)

EAR
Cut pair
dark brown
felt

(labels: L, M)

HEAD GUSSET
Cut 1
oyster felt

(labels: E, E, L, L, J, J, K, K)

SIDE of MOUTH
Cut pair
chocolate
brown

(labels: C, A, D, B)

EYE PIECE
Cut pair
chocolate
brown

(labels: H, B, E, A)

EAR LINING
Cut pair
chocolate brown
felt

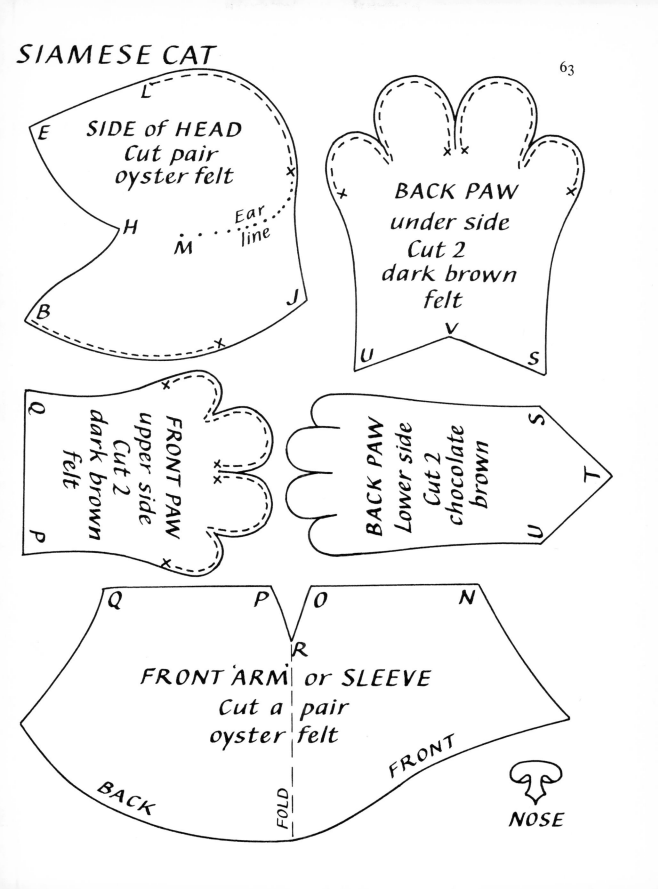

SIAMESE CAT

63

SIDE of HEAD
Cut pair
oyster felt

Ear line

BACK PAW
under side
Cut 2
dark brown
felt

FRONT PAW
upper side
Cut 2
dark brown
felt

BACK PAW
Lower side
Cut 2
chocolate
brown

FRONT ARM or SLEEVE
Cut a pair
oyster felt

BACK

FOLD

FRONT

NOSE

SIAMESE CAT

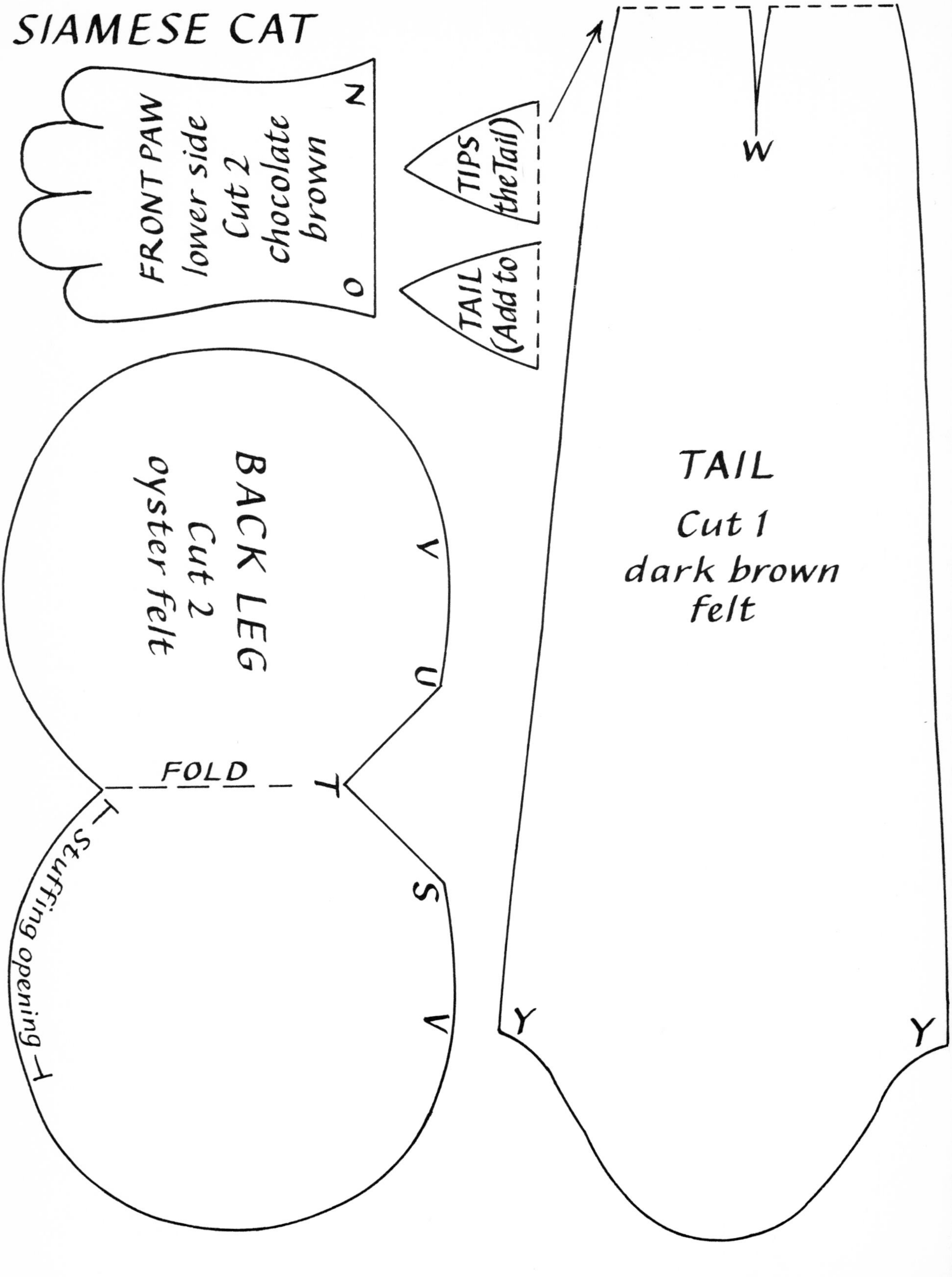

FRONT PAW
lower side
Cut 2
chocolate
brown

N

O

TIPS
(the Tail)

TAIL
(Add to

W

BACK LEG
Cut 2
oyster felt

V

U

FOLD

T

Stuffing opening

S

V

TAIL

Cut 1
dark brown
felt

Y

Y

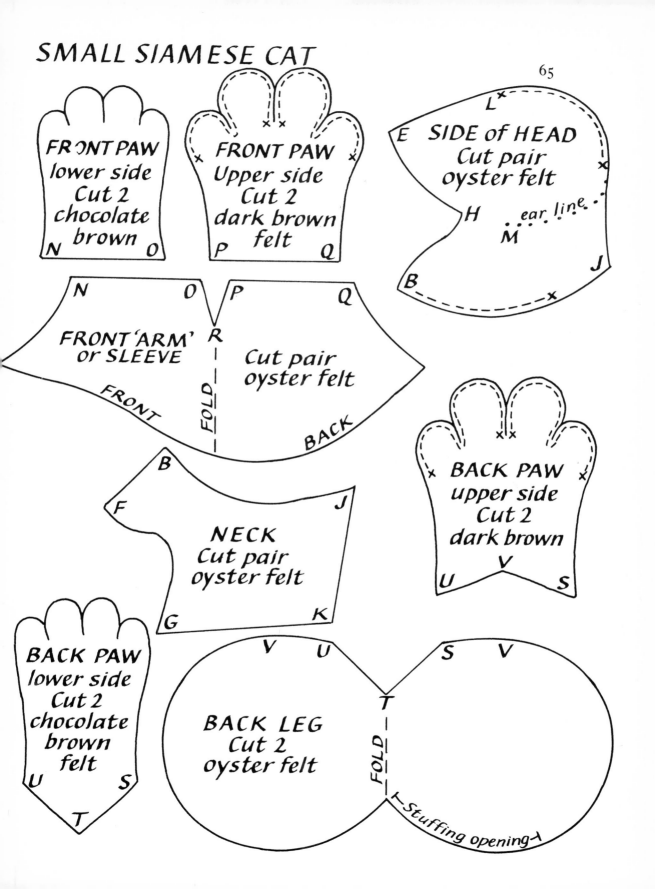

SMALL SIAMESE CAT

65

FRONT PAW
lower side
Cut 2
chocolate
brown

N   O

FRONT PAW
Upper side
Cut 2
dark brown
felt

P   Q

SIDE of HEAD
Cut pair
oyster felt

E
L
H
M   ear line
B
J

N   O   P   Q
R

FRONT 'ARM'
or SLEEVE
FRONT   FOLD   Cut pair
oyster felt
BACK

B
F

NECK
Cut pair
oyster felt

J

G   K

BACK PAW
upper side
Cut 2
dark brown

U   V   S

BACK PAW
lower side
Cut 2
chocolate
brown
felt

U   S
T

V   U   S   V

BACK LEG
Cut 2
oyster felt

T
FOLD

Stuffing opening

SMALL SIAMESE CAT

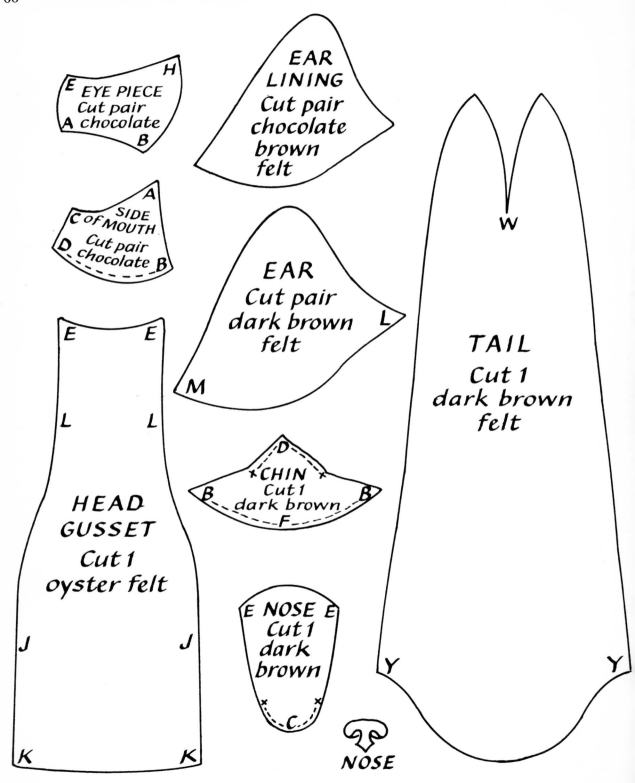

E EYE PIECE
Cut pair **H**
A chocolate
B

EAR LINING
Cut pair
chocolate
brown
felt

A
C SIDE of MOUTH
D Cut pair
chocolate **B**

EAR
Cut pair
dark brown
felt
L
M

E **E**
L **L**

HEAD GUSSET
Cut 1
oyster felt

J **J**

K **K**

D
CHIN
Cut 1
B dark brown **B**
F

E NOSE **E**
Cut 1
dark
brown

C

NOSE

W

TAIL
Cut 1
dark brown
felt

Y **Y**

Siamese Cat: Chart 1   Oyster felt   12″ × 24″

Siamese Cat: Chart 2   Dark brown felt $11'' \times 7\frac{1}{2}''$

Siamese Cat: Chart 3   Light chocolate brown felt $9'' \times 5''$

Materials for the small puppet:

> 10 in. × 20 in. oyster coloured felt for the main parts.
> 9 in. × 6 in. dark brown felt for the ears, nose, chin, paws and tail.
> 7 in. × 4 in. light chocolate brown felt for the remaining brown sections.
> 1 pair blue glass or perspex cat's eyes, size 9 mm.
> Several 12 in. lengths of white or cream horse hair for whiskers.
> A small piece of shiny black gloving leather for eyes and nose.
> A colourless adhesive.
> A 9 inch length of plastic beading or leather, $\frac{3}{8}$ inch wide for the collar.
> Woodwool and rayon filling for the stuffing.

GENERAL INFORMATION

No turnings are required for felt so the stitching should be as near the edges of the felt as possible.

The stitching needs to be fine and firm, without puckering and unless otherwise stated, the seams are open back-stitched on the inside. It is easier to control the seam in gathered sections if the gathers are in front and the seam is double oversewn. Use a matching thread where possible but when two coloured felts are together the main colour is used.

Make the pattern given on pages 62–64 (or 65 and 66 for small puppet) into thin card templates as instructed on page 26. Pierce the dots with a thick needle for the position lines of the ears and back legs, etc.

Lay out the templates for each coloured felt as shown in charts 1, 2, and 3. Mark out closely round the templates, see page 27, and spot through the holes for the position lines on the wrong side of the felt. Cut out each piece very accurately as given on page 27, especially the small pieces. Do not alter the outlines of the patterns as a curved edge is sometimes joined to a straight one, to assist in the modelling of the face. Check all the small pieces of felt after cutting out. Sew in the coloured tacking along the position lines for the ears, etc. (see page 16).

1. THE HEAD

Place out the templates and the corresponding felt pieces for the head as shown in Diagram 1. This will give a better understanding of the assembly and should be used during the make-up of the head.

a. Finely stitch in all the gathering threads marked X . . . X (very near the felt edges) and leave the ends to be adjusted later.

b. Place each eye piece to its adjacent 'side of mouth' piece, A B to A B. Pin at the corners and back-stitch as inside seams.

c. Pin and sew the front seam C D joining the two 'side of mouth' pieces.

d. Still following Diagram 1, place the nose between the 'side of mouth' pieces, pinning E to E and C to C. Adjust the gathers evenly to fit and make a rounded end to the nose (Diagram 2a). Pin and stitch from E to E, round the nose.

e. Pin and sew the neck pieces together F G to F G.

f. First pin the centre of the lower edge of the chin to F on the joined neck pieces. Adjust the gathers so that the chin fits the top of the neck, B F B. Pin and stitch this seam.

g. Next join the front of the head gusset to the nose E to E at both corners and back-stitch this seam across the face.

h. Attach the two 'side of head' pieces to the eye pieces by pinning them together at E H and B. Back-stitch from E to B on each side.

i. Join the 'side of head' pieces to the gusset by pinning them together at J on both sides of the head and again at each end of the gathers. Adjust and pin the gathering threads to fit the 'side of head' pieces to the gusset. Stitch the seam E to J on both sides of the gusset.

j. To attach the chin and neck to the 'side of mouth' pieces, pin them together at B D and B. Adjust the gathers through D on the chin and between D B equally on the 'side of mouth' pieces to produce well curved parts to the front of the face (Diagram 2b). Pin and sew the seam B D B with double oversewing keeping the gathers evenly spaced.

k. Pin the 'side of head' pieces to the neck pieces at J. Adjust the gathers and end the threads. Back-stitch from B to J, oversewing across the gathers. Pin and sew the remaining seam J to K joining the neck to the gusset.

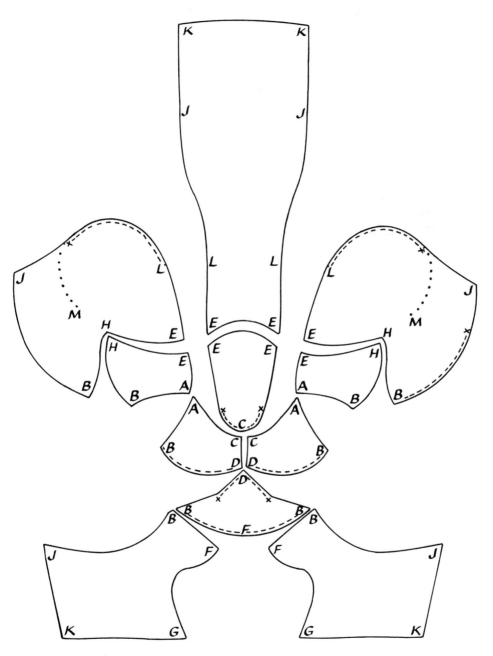

1 *The lay-out of the pattern pieces for the head*

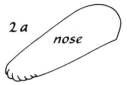

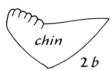

2a

nose

2b

chin

Fullness formed by gathers
to curve the nose and chin

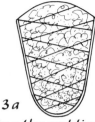

3a

Securing the padding used in
the nose sections, with herring-
bone stitches

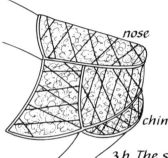

nose

chin

*3b The sections
which are padded
for the modelling
of the face*

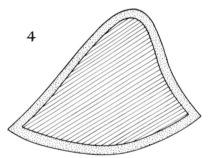

4

The edge of the ear showing
beyond the ear lining

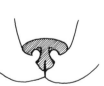

*5   The nose showing
short vertical
stitch on the
centre front*

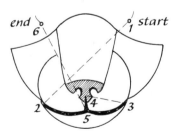

end

6

start

1

2

4

3

5

6   The detached line and numbers
show order and direction of the
embroidery cotton through the
face to form the mouth marks

2. MODELLING AND STUFFING THE HEAD

Before turning the head inside out, each brown section is lightly padded with stuffing level to the seams. Shape and place rayon filling in each brown part and keep it in place with herring-bone stitch. See Diagram 3a and 3b. Turn the head right side out and fill it with cushions of stuffing of rayon and wood-wool as described on page 29. Fill the neck lightly until the finger stall is inserted and then stuff it firmly to the base.

3. THE FINGER-STALL

This is made up from the pattern No. 4 (or No. 7 for small puppet) on pages 35 and 36. Instructions for the make up and insertion of the finger-stall are given on pages 37–39.

4. THE EARS

Make them up as a pair. Stick the linings to the ears with adhesive, smoothly spreading it on the lining only. Place the lining to leave a margin of the dark brown felt round the edge (Diagram 4). Then invisibly sew running stitches just under the edge of the lining to secure it to the ear.

Place each ear in position to the coloured tacking lines on the sides of the head, L M and double ladder-stitch round the back of the ears, neatly and firmly attaching them to the head.

5. THE NOSE AND MOUTH MARKS

Neatly cut a piece of thin black shiny gloving leather to the size of the pattern and with a little adhesive stick it in position as shown in Diagram 5. Ladder stitches passed through the nose and the back of the leather will finally secure the edge in position. Also make a vertical stitch in the centre on the outside of the leather at the base, as shown in Diagram 5. A stitch at each side of the centre will help to define the nostrils.

The Mouth Marks. Using a piece of Anchor soft embroidery cotton with a knot insert the needle in the right eye position and bring it out on the left of the face, as shown in Diagram 6. Work the mouth line stitches allowing the long stitch to lie firmly on the seam between the 'side of mouth' pieces and the chin. The second stitch as shown in the diagram is a short vertical one over the stitch in the centre front of the nose (Diagram 5). End the thread in the left eye position with a stitch and a knot. Both knots will be covered by the eyes eventually.

6. THE EYES

Blue glass or perspex cat's eyes on wires are recommended for this puppet, mounted on shiny black gloving leather.

Pierce the centre of two pieces of black leather, cut the wires behind the eyes to $1\frac{1}{4}$ inches and pass them through the holes. (A little adhesive between the back of the eyes and the leather helps to keep the mounts in place.) With curved scissors, cut the mounts as shown in Diagram 7a and then with round nosed pliers, coil up the wire into double shanks. Refer to page 24 for the instruction for Method II to insert them into the head. (See position in Diagram 7b.)

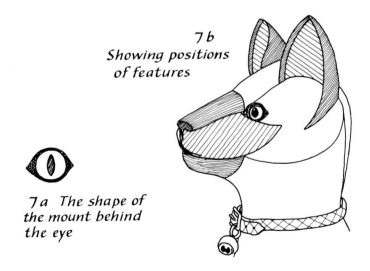

7 b
Showing positions of features

7 a The shape of the mount behind the eye

7. *THE FRONT LEGS OR 'ARMS'*

Make up each to form a pair.

a. Join the lower paw to the 'arm' or sleeve, N O to N O and the upper paw piece to the sleeve P Q to P Q with back-stitching, using dark brown thread.

b. Finely sew in the gathering threads on the upper paw marked X . . . X round the toes, very near the edge of the felt. At the centre of the paw draw up the thread to fit the two toes to the under paw. Fasten off the thread and then continue on round the last two toes and repeat the fitting (see Diagram 8a).

c. Fold the paw right sides together and pin above the wrist seam. Back-stitch from R to the start of the gathers (Diagram 8b) and then double oversew round the toes placing the gathers evenly to fit the under paw. Continue to the end of the gathers and then back-stitch on to the wrist.

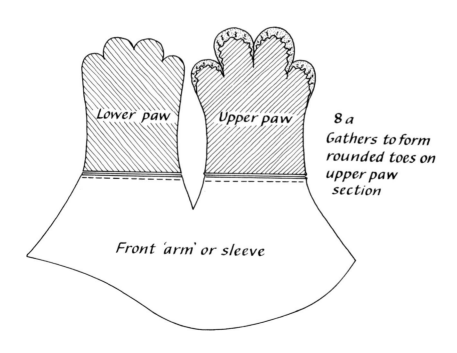

8 a
Gathers to form rounded toes on upper paw section

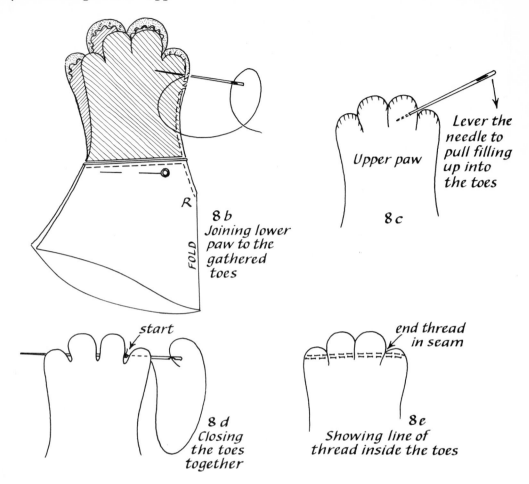

8b
Joining lower
paw to the
gathered
toes

Upper paw

*Lever the
needle to
pull filling
up into
the toes*

8c

start

8d
Closing
the toes
together

end thread
in seam

8e
*Showing line of
thread inside the toes*

d. Turn the paw right side out. (The toes can be pushed outwards with a small stuffing stick.) Lightly stuff with soft filling. Pull a little filling into each toe with a strong needle (see Diagram 8c). Complete the stuffing to the wrist only.

e. Turn the sleeve back over the paw. Place the felt oval within the seam across the wrist and stitch it to the turnings. Turn the sleeve right side out again but do not sew up the remaining seam. It is now ready to insert into the glove.

f. The toes on all four paws can be drawn together if they are too wide apart (see Diagram 8d and 8e).

Make up the second 'arm' in the same way.

8. THE BACK LEGS (*optional*)

To make each leg:

a. Join the lower paw to the back leg, S T U.

b. Follow the instructions for the upper paw gathers in paragraph 7b above.

c. Pin the upper and lower paws together at the corners. Back-stitch from S to the gathers and continue by oversewing round the toes (as for the front paws) and on to U.

d. Turn the paw right side out and wrap the leg sections S V and U V round as shown in Diagram 9 to join to the upper paw S V U. Back-stitch S V and U V and then continue round the leg to the stuffing opening.

e. Turn the leg and lightly stuff the paw, easing some filling into the toes with a needle. Stuff the leg and close the opening with ladder stitch. Flatten the inner side of the leg which is to be the side attached to the glove and well round the outside. After the glove has been made, attach the back legs as shown in Diagram 10 with ladder stitch (see page 17) or a large press stud (see page 21).

f. Draw the toes together if they spread too much.

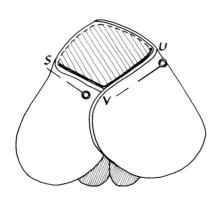

9 *Back leg — joining S.V.U.*
sections the paw

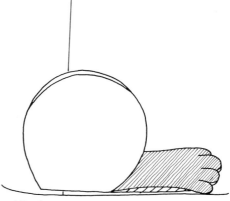

10 *Leg in position over base*
of side seam

9. THE GLOVE

Make up the glove and insert the 'arms' and head from the instructions given on page 30.

10. THE TAIL

Fold the tail in half and back-stitch the seam from W to Y. Turn the tail right side out and very lightly stuff with soft filling. Attach it to the centre back of the puppet at the base of the glove.

11. THE WHISKERS

Real horse hair is more suitable as whiskers than man-made fibres. Lengths of 12 inches or longer can be used, threaded into a needle and sewn through the nose until the ends of hair are secure when pulled from either side. Full instructions are given on page 19.

12. THE COLLAR

Various plastic beadings are obtainable (at home decorators) which are suitable for collars. Attach a small buckle to one end of the beading, securing it with a bifurcated paper clip as shown in Diagram 11 and cut the other end as shown in the same diagram. A small bell can be fixed to the collar as a suitable addition. (See page 20.)

11   *Collar with buckle attached*

The Fox Terrier

A Fox Terrier puppet can be used as a companion for the Clown and the opportunity has also been taken to introduce an animal with the attraction of an open mouth, for which the Terrier is particularly suitable. This does not entail much extra work and when voices are used with the puppets the open mouth supports the illusion that the dog is actually speaking. Alternative instructions are given for a closed mouth if this is preferred.

A smaller size Terrier pattern has been included on pages 86–88. This might be preferred as being more related in size to the Clown when the two appear together and makes possible its use for play between an adult and a child. As an accessory when in the role of the Clown's companion, a ruff can be used instead of a collar for which the pattern is given. Also a felt doggy jacket for alternative use and as a colourful extra.

Materials required for the full size puppet:

12 in. × 27 in. white felt.

8 in. × 6 in. black felt.

5 in. × 6 in. flesh pink felt for the open mouth.

$1\frac{1}{2}$ in. × $2\frac{1}{2}$ in. rose pink felt for the open mouth.

12 in. × 1 in. piece of soft black gloving leather with a shiny surface for the nose and mouth.

10 in. thin string.

A pair of 13 mm. brown eyes or Dog's eyes (on wire).

A 10 in. length of plastic beading or leather, $\frac{1}{2}$ in. wide for the collar.

A small tube of U.H.U. or similar colourless adhesive.

Stuffing—a mixture of rayon or similar soft filling and woodwool.

Materials for the small puppet:

10 in. × 21 in. white felt.

6 in. × $5\frac{1}{2}$ in. black felt.

(*Continued on page 91*)

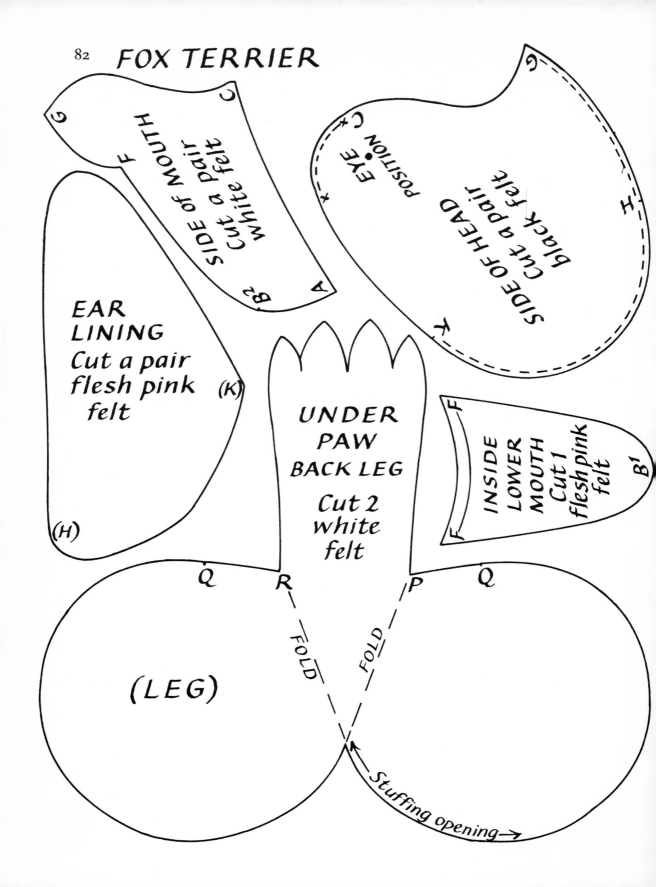

82 FOX TERRIER

SIDE of MOUTH
Cut a Pair
white felt

SIDE of HEAD
Cut a pair
black felt

EYE
POSITION

EAR
LINING
Cut a pair
flesh pink
felt

(K)

(H)

UNDER
PAW
BACK LEG

Cut 2
white
felt

INSIDE
LOWER
MOUTH
Cut 1
flesh pink
felt

(LEG)

FOLD

FOLD

Stuffing opening →

FOX TERRIER

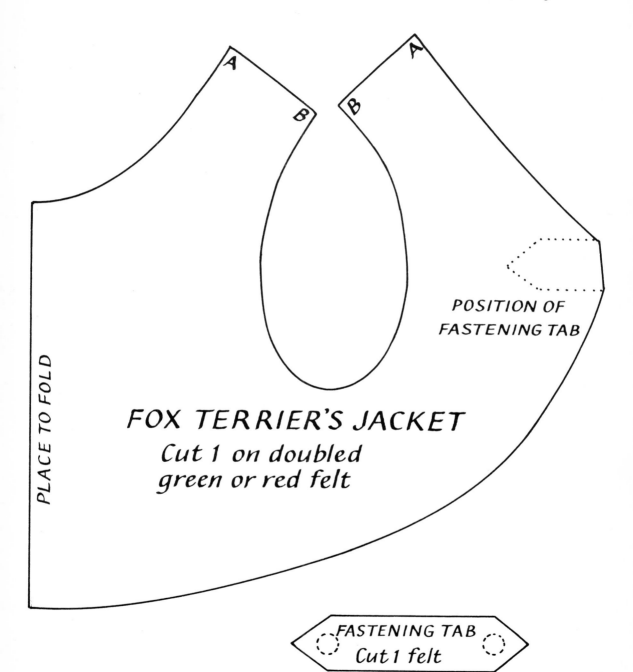

A

B

B

A

POSITION OF
FASTENING TAB

PLACE TO FOLD

FOX TERRIER'S JACKET
Cut 1 on doubled
green or red felt

FASTENING TAB
Cut 1 felt

FOX TERRIER

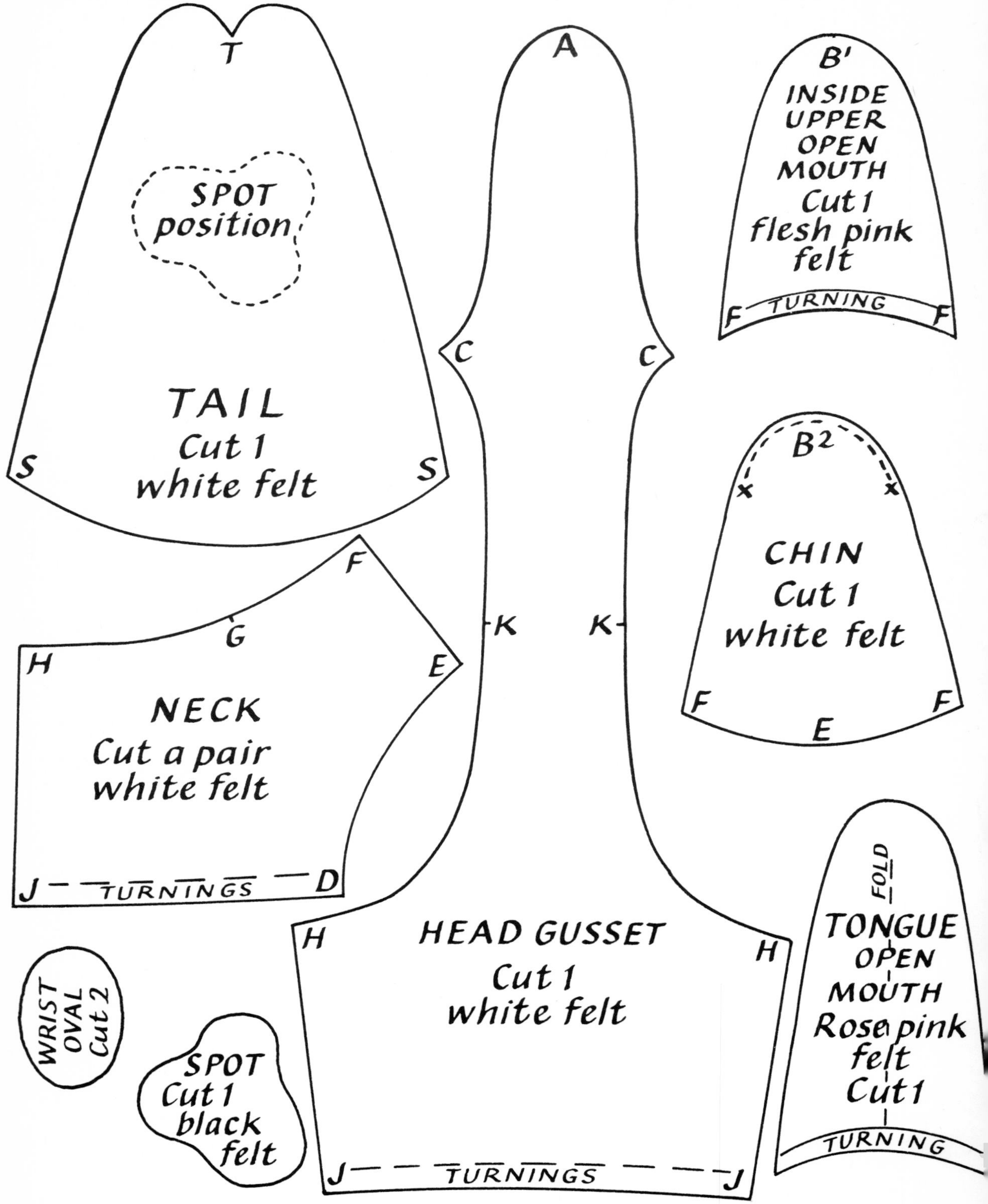

T

TAIL
Cut 1
white felt

SPOT position

S S

A

C C

K K

NECK
Cut a pair
white felt

F
G
E
H

J — TURNINGS — D

B'
INSIDE UPPER OPEN MOUTH
Cut 1
flesh pink felt

F TURNING F

B²
X X

CHIN
Cut 1
white felt

F F
E

HEAD GUSSET
Cut 1
white felt

H H

WRIST OVAL Cut 2

SPOT
Cut 1
black felt

J — — TURNINGS — — J

TONGUE OPEN MOUTH
Rose pink felt
Cut 1

FOLD

TURNING

FOX TERRIER

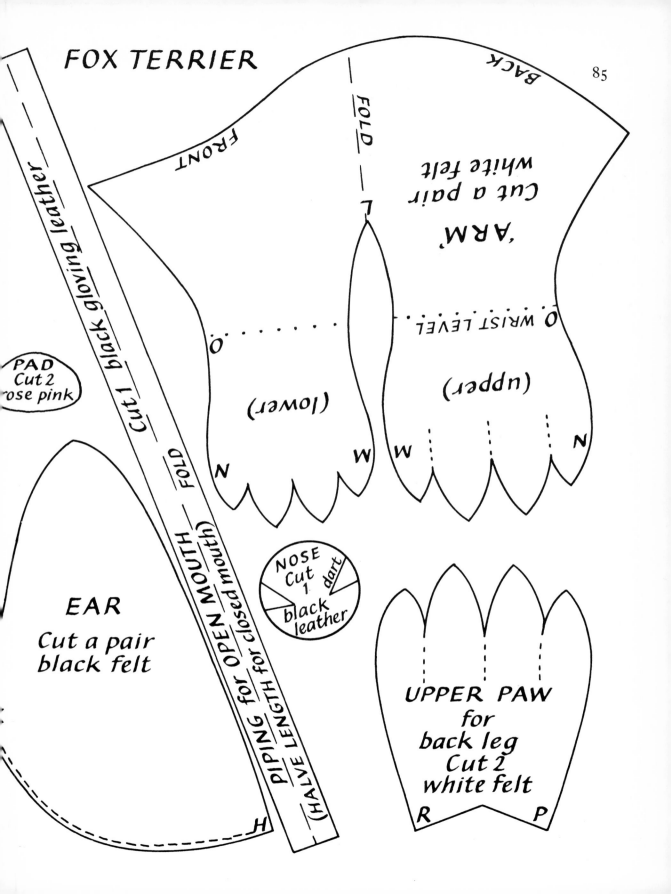

FRONT

FOLD

BACK

ARM'
Cut a pair
white felt

O. WRIST LEVEL

(upper)

(lower)

Cut 1 black gloving leather

FOLD

PAD
Cut 2
rose pink

PIPING for OPEN MOUTH
(HALVE LENGTH for closed mouth)

NOSE
Cut
1
dart
black
leather

EAR

Cut a pair
black felt

UPPER PAW
for
back leg
Cut 2
white felt

SMALL FOX TERRIER

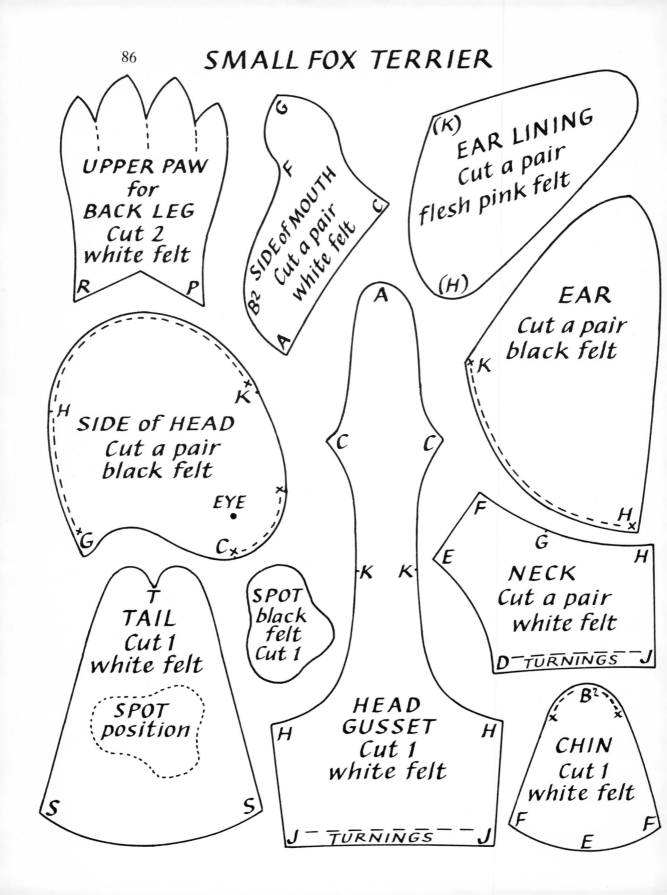

UPPER PAW
for
BACK LEG
Cut 2
white felt

SIDE of MOUTH
Cut a pair
white felt

(K) EAR LINING
Cut a pair
flesh pink felt

EAR
Cut a pair
black felt

SIDE of HEAD
Cut a pair
black felt

EYE

NECK
Cut a pair
white felt

TURNINGS

TAIL
Cut 1
white felt

SPOT
position

SPOT
black
felt
Cut 1

HEAD
GUSSET
Cut 1
white felt

TURNINGS

CHIN
Cut 1
white felt

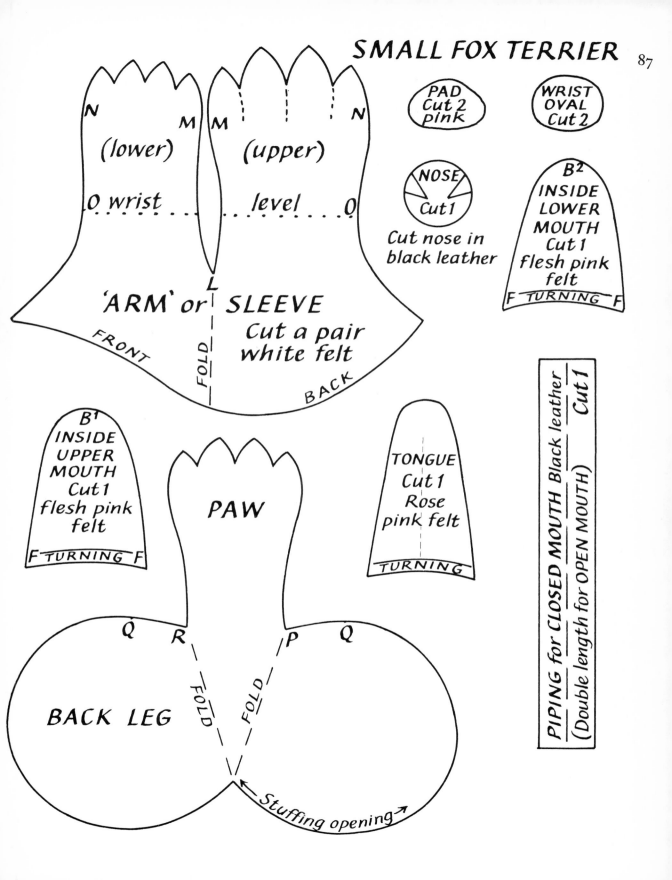

N M M N

(lower) (upper)

O wrist level O

'ARM' or SLEEVE
Cut a pair
white felt

FRONT

FOLD

L

BACK

PAD
Cut 2
pink

WRIST
OVAL
Cut 2

NOSE
Cut 1

Cut nose in
black leather

B²
INSIDE
LOWER
MOUTH
Cut 1
flesh pink
felt

F TURNING F

B¹
INSIDE
UPPER
MOUTH
Cut 1
flesh pink
felt

F TURNING F

PAW

TONGUE
Cut 1
Rose
pink felt

TURNING

PIPING for CLOSED MOUTH Black leather Cut 1
(Double length for OPEN MOUTH)

Q R P Q

FOLD FOLD

BACK LEG

Stuffing opening

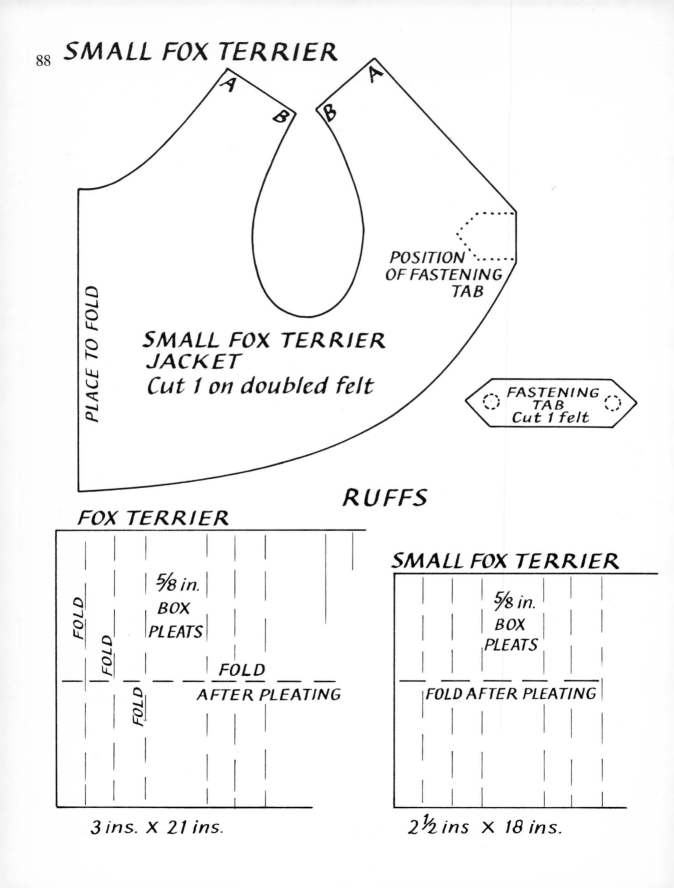

SMALL FOX TERRIER

A

B

B

A

POSITION
OF FASTENING
TAB

PLACE TO FOLD

SMALL FOX TERRIER
JACKET
Cut 1 on doubled felt

FASTENING
TAB
Cut 1 felt

RUFFS

FOX TERRIER

5⁄8 in.
BOX
PLEATS

FOLD

FOLD

FOLD

FOLD

FOLD
AFTER PLEATING

3 ins. X 21 ins.

SMALL FOX TERRIER

5⁄8 in.
BOX
PLEATS

FOLD AFTER PLEATING

2½ ins X 18 ins.

Fox Terrier:
Chart 1   White felt
     12″ × 27″

90

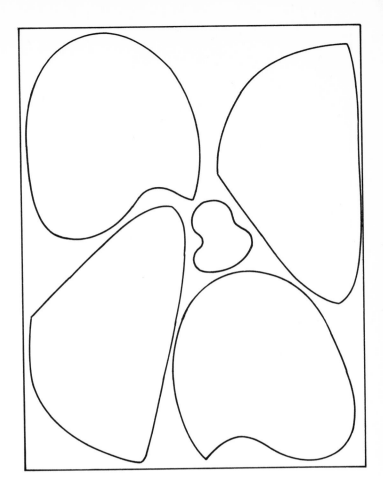

Fox Terrier:
Chart 2   Black felt
   8″ × 6″

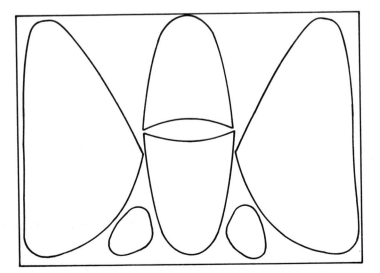

Chart 3   Flesh pink felt
      5″ × 6″

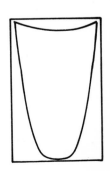

Chart 4   Rose felt
$2\frac{1}{2}″ × 1\frac{1}{2}″$

4 in. × 4½ in. flesh pink felt, for the open mouth.

2 in. × 1¼ in. rose pink felt, for the open mouth.

8 in. × 1 in. soft black gloving leather with a shiny surface for the nose and mouth.

6 in. of thin string.

A pair of 9 mm. brown glass eyes or Dog's eyes (on wire).

A 9 in. length of plastic beading or leather ½ inch wide, for the collar.
Adhesive and stuffing as above.

GENERAL INFORMATION

To make up the puppet with a closed mouth in either the large or small size, omit Section 1A and use Section 1B which follows it, otherwise the instructions are the same for both puppets.

No turnings are required on the felt for these puppets.

The seams are on the inside and worked in open back-stitch, except in certain places where double oversewing is recommended. Stitch as near the edges as possible after pinning the beginning and ends of the seams, and between as necessary. Sew firmly but without puckering the work. Reference should be made to the technical points in pages 9–41.

Make the pattern on pages 82–85 into thin card templates as described on page 26 and pierce the dotted lines with a thick needle.

Place the templates on the felts, arranging them as suggested on the 4 Charts.

Mark and cut out as instructed on page 27. Mark the start and the end of the gathered sections and the dotted lines (through the needle holes) on the back of the felts. Mark the exact position of the eyes on the *right* side of the black felt with coloured cotton.

1A. MAKE-UP OF THE HEAD WITH AN OPEN MOUTH

a. Lay out the templates and the felt pieces as shown in Diagram 1. Tack an 'L' on the lower mouth piece for easy identification. Put the tongue between the upper and lower mouth pieces and sew the three thicknesses together with back-stitching along the back of the mouth pieces, 1/16 inch from the edges (Diagram 2a). The shape of the tongue is

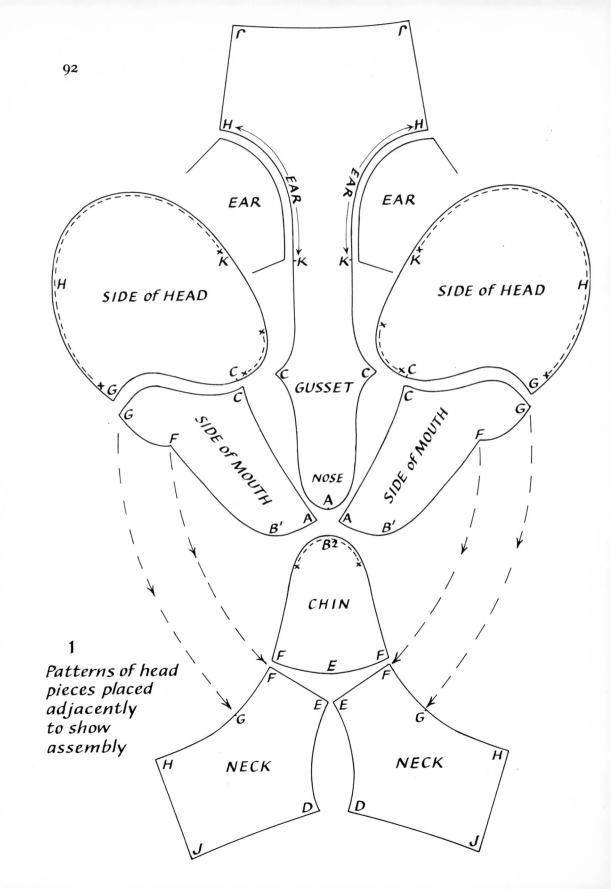

92

EAR

EAR

SIDE of HEAD

SIDE of HEAD

GUSSET

SIDE of MOUTH

SIDE of MOUTH

NOSE

CHIN

1

Patterns of head
pieces placed
adjacently
to show
assembly

NECK

NECK

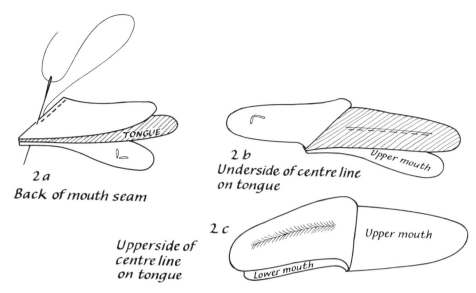

2a
Back of mouth seam

2b
Underside of centre line on tongue

2c
Upperside of centre line on tongue

improved by fairly loosely stab-stitching a centre line along the underside of the tongue (see pattern). Start and end the stab-stitching invisibly and without knots (Diagram 2b and 2c).

b. Following Diagram 1, pin and sew together the two 'side of head' pieces, A to B^1. To this add the front part of the head gusset, A to A. Pin and sew A–C on each 'side of mouth' piece to A–C on the gusset.

c. Sew in the gathering thread between X . . . X on the chin piece with fine running stitches near the edge of the felt. Pull up the gathers to form a good curve to the front of the chin, and end the thread securely (Diagram 3a and 3b).

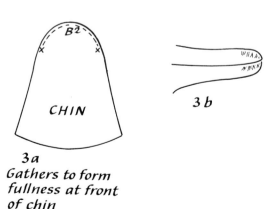

3a
Gathers to form fullness at front of chin

3b

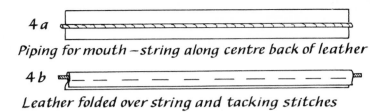

4a
Piping for mouth – string along centre back of leather

4b
Leather folded over string and tacking stitches

d. Join the neck pieces together at the front seam D to E as shown in Diagram 1. Add the chin piece placing E to E and F to F at each corner and stitch F E F.

e. The piping is now prepared for the black edges of the open mouth, using the 9 inch strip of leather, and piece of string. Trail a thin line of adhesive from the tube along the centre of the back of the leather strip and place the string along the adhesive (Diagram 4a). Press it on firmly and then fold the leather in half lengthways over the string as tightly as possible, keeping the edges level. With $\frac{1}{4}$ inch stitches sew in a white tacking thread, $\frac{1}{8}$ inch from the outside of the folded edge (Diagram 4b). (Be exact with this measurement as it will be an important guide line when sewing the piping to the mouth pieces.)

f. Next attach the piping to the upper and lower mouth pieces. First fold and pin the tongue on to the lower mouth piece to avoid including it in the stitching (Diagram 5). Following Diagram 6a which shows the two mouth pieces open with the centre seam uppermost, place the piping behind the mouth on the far side of the seam, with the cut edges upwards. Back-stitch the mouth to the piping with flesh pink cotton keeping the stitching $\frac{1}{16}$ inch below the edge of the flesh pink felt. (It is essential to stab this back-stitch to be able to watch the back as well as the front of the seam to keep an even line.) About an inch from the end,

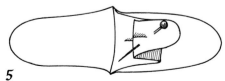

5
Tongue folded away from stitch lines

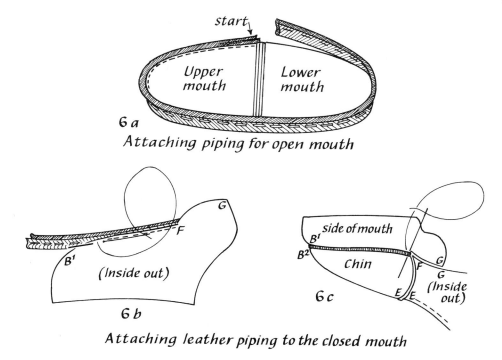

6a
Attaching piping for open mouth

6b
Attaching leather piping to the closed mouth

measure the length required and reduce the piping if necessary so that the ends just meet—edge to edge without overlapping. Invisibly join the two ends of piping with black thread, and finish the seam.

g. Pin the two 'side of mouth' pieces F G to the neck pieces F G and stitch these two short seams.

h. To attach the open mouth to the chin and 'side of mouth' pieces, follow Diagram 7. Hold the mouth with the piping uppermost and the tongue (still pinned to the lower mouth) to the left. Place the chin piece above the lower mouth and tongue and place the seam F E F above the seam across the back of the mouth as shown in the diagram. Pin the front of the chin (B^2) to the centre front of the lower mouth at B^2 and pin at F on each side of the chin piece to the ends of the seam across the back of the mouth. Place the 'side of mouth' pieces over the upper mouth and pin both together at B^2. The mouth should fit into the face exactly.

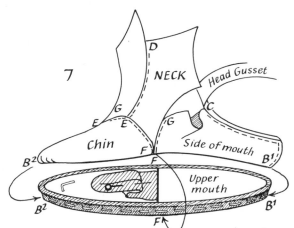

Attaching the open mouth parts to the nose and chin sections – shown inside out above the mouth

i. Starting at F with a white thread, back-stitch round the entire edge of the chin and 'side of mouth' pieces, keeping the stitching $\frac{1}{16}$ inch below the edge of the felt and above the tacking on the piping. Stab the back-stitching through all the thicknesses and over the row of pink back-stitching on the edge of the mouth pieces. Turn the upper and lower parts of the mouth right sides out. Remove the 'L' from the lower mouth. The upper mouth only should be again turned inside out and pushed into the unturned lower mouth so that it is out of the way while working on the rest of the head. Turn the head gusset and the neck inside out, ready to continue the seams of the head.

j. Pin both the H J edges at the back of the gusset to the two H J parts of the neck pieces and stitch these seams. This closes the neck and leaves the space on each side for the black 'side of head' pieces and the ears which are made next.

The instructions for Section 2 should now be followed to complete the puppet.

1B. HEAD WITHOUT AN OPEN MOUTH

(This section is used instead of 1A.)

Place the templates on the appropriate felt pieces for the head and arrange as shown in Diagram 1 (page 92) to show the assembly of the parts.

a. Place the two 'side of mouth' pieces, right sides together, pin and back-stitch the front seam A–B¹ exactly.

b. To this add the front of the head gusset, securing A to A. Pin C to C on each side of the gusset and sew the two A C seams.

c. Sew in a gathering thread between X . . . X on the chin with fine stitches near the edge. Pull up the gathers to form a curve to the front of the chin (Diagram 3a and 3b) and end securely.

d. Pin and sew together the two neckpieces from D to E.

e. Add the chin piece to the neck, pinning and sewing F E F.

f. The piping for the outline of the mouth is prepared from the strip of leather and piece of string. Trail a thin line of adhesive from the tube along the centre back of the leather strip. Place the string on it and roll the strip in half, lengthways over the string (Diagrams 4a and 4b). Press well together. With $\frac{1}{4}$ inch stitches sew in a white tacking cotton (not more than $\frac{1}{8}$ inch from the folded edge) through the two thicknesses of the piping. Be accurate as this tacking will act as a guide line when sewing the piping to the felt pieces.

g. To attach the prepared piping, place it along the 'side of mouth' pieces against the 'right' side of the felt from F to B¹ to F, keeping the felt edge below the piping edges (Diagram 6b). From F back-stitch as near the felt edge as possible through one or both thicknesses of the leather between the tacking line and the string in the piping. Make the latter as narrow as possible on the outside. End the thread securely at F on the other side of the mouth but do not cut it off. Put the needle and thread straight back through the piping at F ready to attach the chin.

h. Pin the chin to the piping at F on each side and pin B² to B¹ at the centre front (Diagram 6c). With the chin towards the worker, stab a line of back-stitching between the tacking and the string in the piping. Work near the edge of the felt from F to B² to F, taking the needle right through the piping to the row of stitching along the felt 'side of mouth' piece.

i. Pin the 'side of mouth' pieces from F to G to the neck F G and stitch these short seams.

j. Pin and sew the H J seams joining the back of the gusset to the neck—which leaves a space to contain the black 'side of head' pieces and the ears.

2. THE MAKE-UP OF THE EARS

It is advisable to use white thread for the remaining stitching of the head seams.

Sew in the gathering threads between X . . . X on each ear. Pull up the gathers so that the base of the ear H K fits H K on the back of the gusset. Pin the ears in position on the gusset, H to H and K to K, placing the gathers evenly between these two points. Oversew the ears to the gusset. (After attaching them it is easier to put each ear inside the head and let them remain there until the head is completed). The linings are added after the head is finished and turned.

Inserting the 'side of head' pieces.

a. First sew in the gathering thread between K H and G, and at C on the 'side of head' pieces, and leave the threads to adjust later.

b. Follow the lay-out of the pattern pieces in Diagram 1 and place the 'side of head' and the 'side of mouth' pieces together G to G and C to C, and back-stitch these seams.

c. On each 'side of head' piece pull up the gathers well at C and end the threads securely. Place K C on both 'side of head' pieces to K C on each side of the gusset. Pin and stitch these seams. Adjust the gathers evenly, fitting H K on the 'side of head' to H K on the gusset and pin together. Continue by fitting and pinning the 'side of head' to the neck pieces, H G to H G distributing the gathers evenly. Back-stitch the G H K seams, stabbing the stitching along the section H K where there are three thicknesses of felt. (Keep the gathering thread and oversewing on the turnings.) This completes the head seams, and the head *without* an open mouth should be turned right side out.

d. For the *head with an open mouth*, take the lower mouth out of the upper mouth and turn the head right side out. In order to keep the mouth from

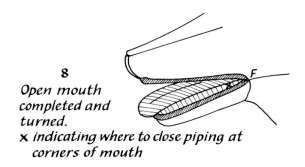

8

*Open mouth
completed and
turned.*
x *indicating where to close piping at
corners of mouth*

opening too much at the corners, ladder-stitch the piping together for $\frac{1}{4}$ inch from F on each side at the back of the mouth (Diagram 8).

3. THE FINGER-STALL

Make this up from the pattern No. 4 (or No. 7 for small puppet), pages 35 and 36 as instructed on page 37. When the stuffing of the head (as given in the next section), is completed, insert and attach it as directed on page 39.

4. STUFFING THE HEAD

Make cushions of rayon and woodwool evenly mixed as instructed on page 29. Firstly fit cushions of the shape required into the lower and upper mouth. Fill the top of the head and then the cheeks, fitting the cushions well into the gathered sections to model the face. Add more filling in any spaces between the cushions and continue stuffing the neck in conjunction with the insertion of the finger-stall from the directions on page 39.

5. THE NOSE

a. Using the soft black leather with the shiny side outwards, cut out the nose piece exactly to the size of the pattern. Fold the two darts to form the nostrils as shown in Diagram 9a and 9b and secure each dart with a stitch at the edge. Pin the nose piece to fit snugly over the front end of the head.

b. With a thread of black Anchor soft embroidery cotton make a vertical

9 a

9 b

Folding the leather as
darts for the nostrils

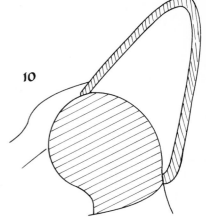

10

9 c — piping

The made-up nose piece pinned to the
head and showing the central stitch
joining the nose to the piping

Position of the ear lining leaving
black edge round the ear

stitch from the piping at the centre front over the seam A B^1, to end on
the leather nose as shown in Diagram 9c.

c. Next attach the nose to the head with adhesive and invisible stitching.

6. TO ATTACH EACH EAR LINING

a. Place a pink felt ear lining inside an ear and pin together across the
centre, leaving a margin of black felt showing evenly beyond the edges
of the lining (Diagram 10).

b. Starting at the tip, apply adhesive thinly to the back of the top half of
the lining and press the lining and the ear firmly together. Treat the
lower half in the same way. Avoid showing any adhesive on the black
felt edges.

c. Before the adhesive dries, curve the ear forward into a natural position.
If necessary secure the tip to the head, $\frac{1}{4}$–$\frac{1}{2}$ inch behind the outside
corner of the eye with a small stitch. Line the other ear in the same way.

11 a

Backing of white felt
cut to points at the
corners

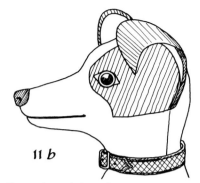

11 b

Completed head showing position
of eyes and ears etc.

7. THE EYES

Glass eyes on wires are used for this puppet.

   a. Cut the wire to leave $1\frac{1}{4}$ inch behind each eye. Pierce the centre of two small pieces of white felt with a thick needle. Put a little adhesive into the back of each eye and pass the wires through the holes in the felt. Press the felt to the back of the eyes.

   b. With curved scissors cut the felt level with the glass above and below each eye and point each corner as shown in Diagram 11a. Using round nosed pliers, coil up the wire into a double shank, ending close to the eye as shown in Diagram 17b page 22. Insert the eyes as instructed for Method II page 24, placing them as indicated in Diagram 11b.

   If dog's eyes with white corners are used, a circle only of white felt, without corners, is recommended. (White felt gives brightness to brown eyes.)

8. THE LEGS AND PAWS

The paws on the 'arms' and on the back legs are worked in the same way. It will be noticed that the upper felt for the paws is larger than the under one. This is to allow more fullness on the top of the paws.

   a. *The front legs or 'arms'.* First fold the felt, right sides together, along

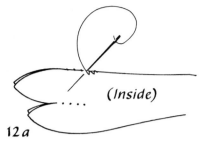

12 a

*Oversewing the folded lines
for the divisions of the toes*

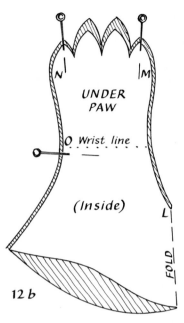

UNDER
PAW

O Wrist line

(Inside)

FOLD

12 b

*'Arm' or sleeve and paw
prepared for stitching*

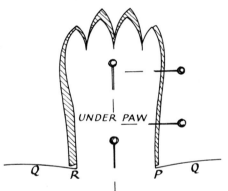

UNDER PAW

Q   R   P   Q

12 c *Back leg prepared for
stitching*

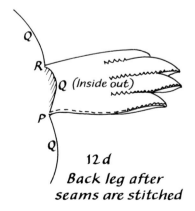

Q

R

Q *(Inside out)*

P

Q

12 d
*Back leg after
seams are stitched*

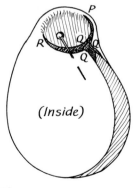

P

R   Q   Q

Q

(Inside)

12 e

*Back paw with leg
wrapped round for the
P. Q. R. seam*

each short dotted line on the upper paws and double oversew over each fold, working towards the slits (Diagram 12a).

b. Fold each 'arm' right sides together and pin as in Diagram 12b. Back-stitch from L to M then double oversew round the toes, keeping the tips level and easing the larger edges of the upper felt to fit the smaller lower edges of the paw. Back-stitch from N to O.

c. Turn the paws and stuff each with soft filling to the wrist line only, well pointing the toes. (The filling can be eased into the toes with a strong needle from the outside. See page 29 and Diagram 22.)

d. Insert and stitch in the oval wrist felts to secure the stuffing in the paws, and leave the remaining seam from the wrist to the armhole to be sewn later.

e. *The back legs.* To make each leg, the toes are worked in the same way as from L M N O on the front legs or 'arms'. Start the stitching at P and sew round the toes to R, as shown in Diagram 12c and 12d.

f. Turn the paw right side out and wrap the leg sections P Q and R Q round as shown in Diagram 12e. Back-stitch P Q R and then stitch from Q round the leg to the stuffing opening.

g. Turn the leg and lightly stuff the paw with rayon filling, well pointing the toes, then fill the leg and close the stuffing opening with ladder stitch. Flatten the inner side of the leg which is the side to be attached to the glove and leave the outer side rounded.

h. To complete the toes on all four paws, stab-stitch vertically over the stitched folds between the toes from the upper to the lower felts—just

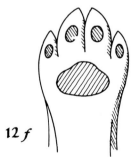

12 f

Under paw showing shape and position of felt pads

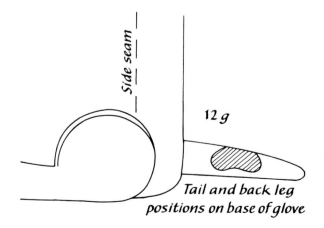

12 g

Tail and back leg positions on base of glove

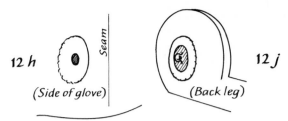

Attachment of felt circles to mask large press studs for detachable back legs

sufficiently to emphasise the division of the toes, and end the threads invisibly. Pieces of rose, black or pink felt can be stuck and invisibly stitched to the lower side of the paws (arranged as shown in Diagram 12f), to suggest pads.

9. THE GLOVE AND LEGS

To make up the glove and insert the 'arms' and head follow the instructions given on page 30.

The back legs are added to the base of the glove just forward of the side seams and level with the base (see Diagram 12g). Ladder-stitch them securely to the outside of the glove. If detachable back legs are preferred use a large press fastener for each leg as shown in Diagrams 12h and 12j. Instructions are given on page 21.

10. THE TAIL

Fold the tail in half lengthways and pin and stitch the inside seam from S to T. Turn it and lightly stuff. Attach the spot with adhesive to the tail in the position marked on the pattern and invisibly stitch it in place. Attach the tail to the base of the glove in the centre back with the seam downwards. Ladder-stitch securely in place (Diagram 12g).

11. THE COLLAR

A variety of $\frac{1}{2}$ inch wide plastic beading can be obtained (from home decorators) which makes attractive collars. Attach a suitable buckle to one end with a small bifurcated paper clip and pierce small holes to the shaped end as in Diagram 13. Alternatively a narrow belt can be adapted to the size required.

12. THE JACKET

Materials required:

> 6 in. × 12 in. bright coloured felt.
> 48 in. Russia or similar braid.

This is a simple doggy jacket, the only seams being those on the shoulders. It is fastened in front with buttons or press studs, attaching the tab to close the jacket. A narrow edging such as a Russia braid in a contrasting colour can be applied as an attractive decoration.

The Small Fox Terrier requires:

> 5 in. × $9\frac{1}{2}$ in. felt.
> 1 yard Russia braid.

Make up this jacket as above.

13. THE RUFF (*used without the jacket*)

This 7 inch box pleated ruff requires:

> 3 in. × 21 in. Tarlatan or similar stiffened material.
> $\frac{1}{2}$ yard Russia braid.

Follow the fold marks given on the pattern, making $\frac{5}{8}$ inch box pleats and make up the ruff from the instructions given for the Clown's ruff on page 168.

The Small Fox Terrier's Ruff needs:

> $2\frac{1}{2}$ in. × 18 in. Tarlatan.
> $\frac{1}{2}$ yard Russia braid.

This $5\frac{1}{2}$ inch ruff is made up from the above instructions, with the same size box pleats.

13 The collar – showing use of bi-furcated paper clip to secure buckle to strap

Dinah Duck

This is one of the 'feathered' group of glove puppets, made in fur fabric materials to simulate a feathered effect.

The design is practical and an attractive natural shape. It allows a wide degree of manipulation on any suitable surface, and the legs and feet are designed to permit a convincing stance with appropriate flexible movements, while the short straight finger-stall allows the beak to reach ground level and under the wings.

Materials required:

> 12 in. × 24 in. white nylon fur fabric, for body and wings. (Stroke of pile in 24 in. direction.)
> 6 in. × 5 in. white felt for the wing edges and finger-stall.
> 6 in × 6 in. orange felt for feet and beak.
> 6 in × 7 in. Iron-on Vilene to stiffen the undertail and wings.
> 3 in. × 7 in. green felt for collar.
> A thread of six-stranded orange embroidery cotton.
> A pair of 13 mm. brown glass or perspex eyes.
> 4 pipe cleaners.
> 16 in. white $\frac{1}{2}$ in. tape or bias binding for wing openings.
> 9 in. red Russia braid or $\frac{1}{2}$ in. ribbon for collar bow.
> A tube of U.H.U. or similar adhesive.
> Stuffing, a mixture of rayon filling and woodwool, for the head.

GENERAL INFORMATION

Allow $\frac{1}{4}$ inch turnings beyond the marking out line on the fur fabric. Turnings on felt are not necessary unless indicated on the pattern piece concerned.
Stitching (see also page 13). All seams on the body and head are open back-stitched on the inside, and sewing should be done just inside the marking out line. The pieces for the beak and legs are stab-stitched on the outside near

(*Continued on page 113*)

DINAH DUCK

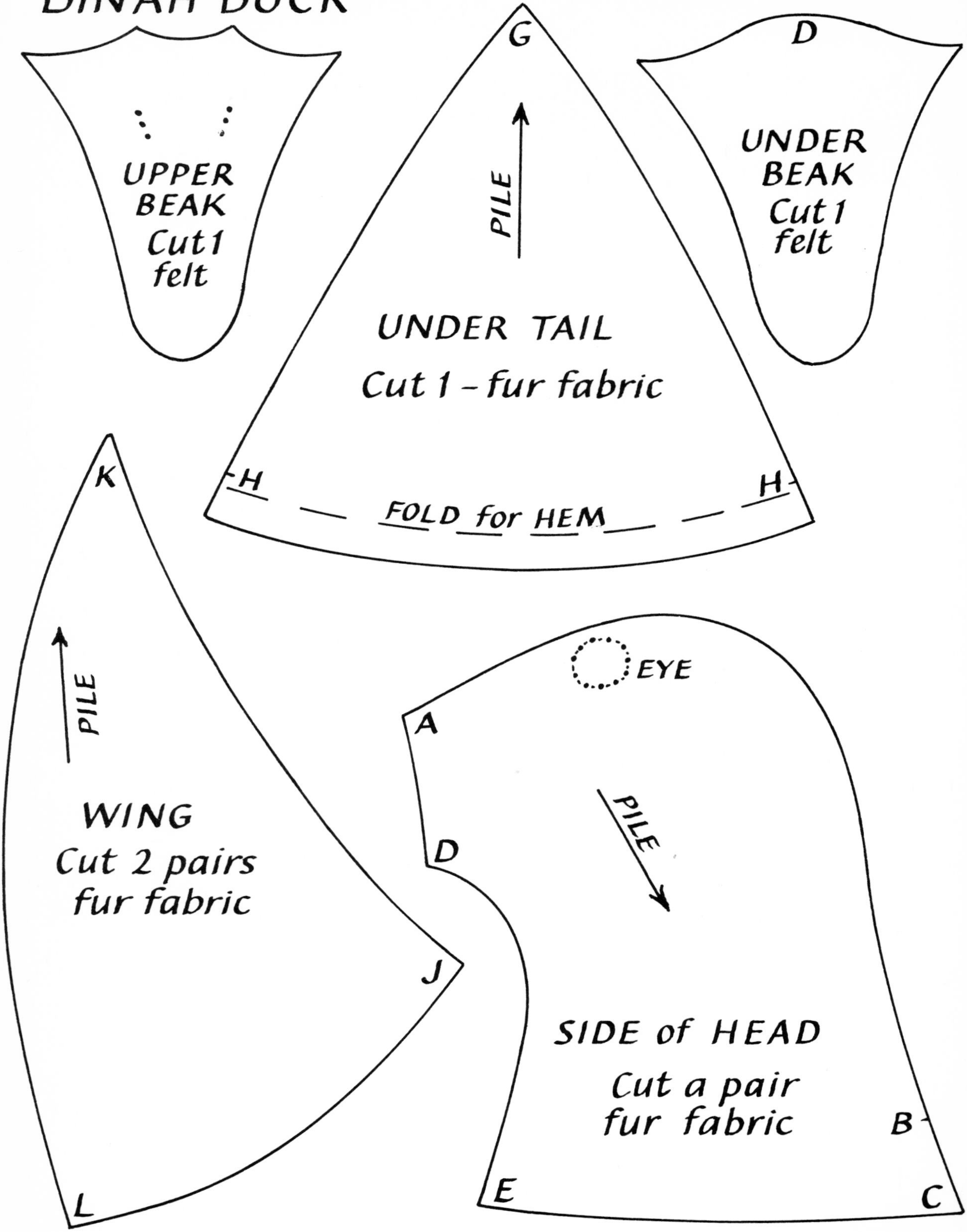

UPPER BEAK
Cut 1
felt

UNDER BEAK
Cut 1
felt

UNDER TAIL
Cut 1 – fur fabric

PILE

G

D

H

H

FOLD for HEM

WING
Cut 2 pairs
fur fabric

PILE

K

J

L

EYE

PILE

A

D

J

SIDE of HEAD
Cut a pair
fur fabric

B

E

C

DINAH DUCK

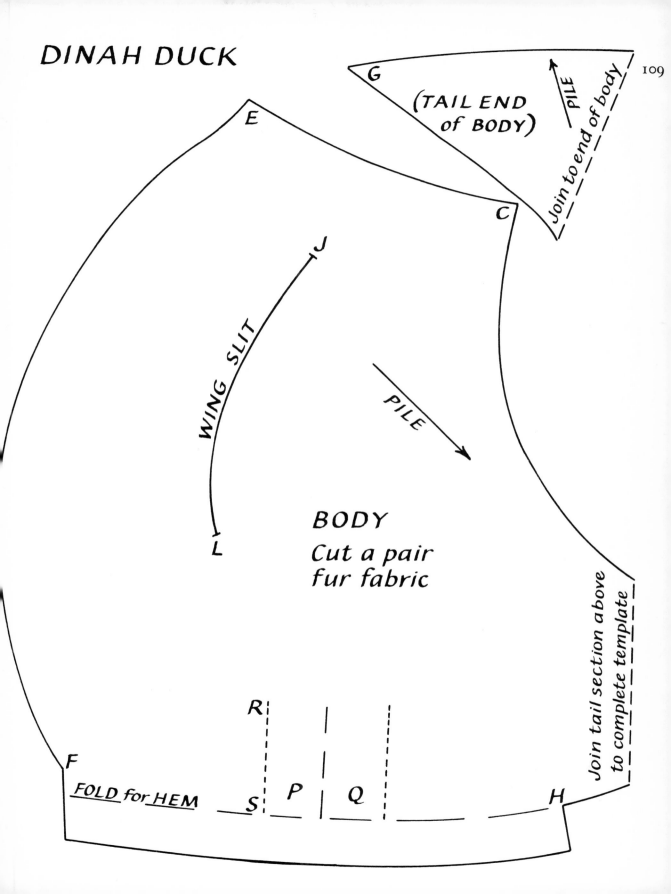

G

E

(TAIL END of BODY)

PILE

Join to end of body

C

J

WING SLIT

PILE

L

BODY
Cut a pair
fur fabric

Join tail section above to complete template

R

F

FOLD for HEM

S   P   Q

H

DINAH DUCK

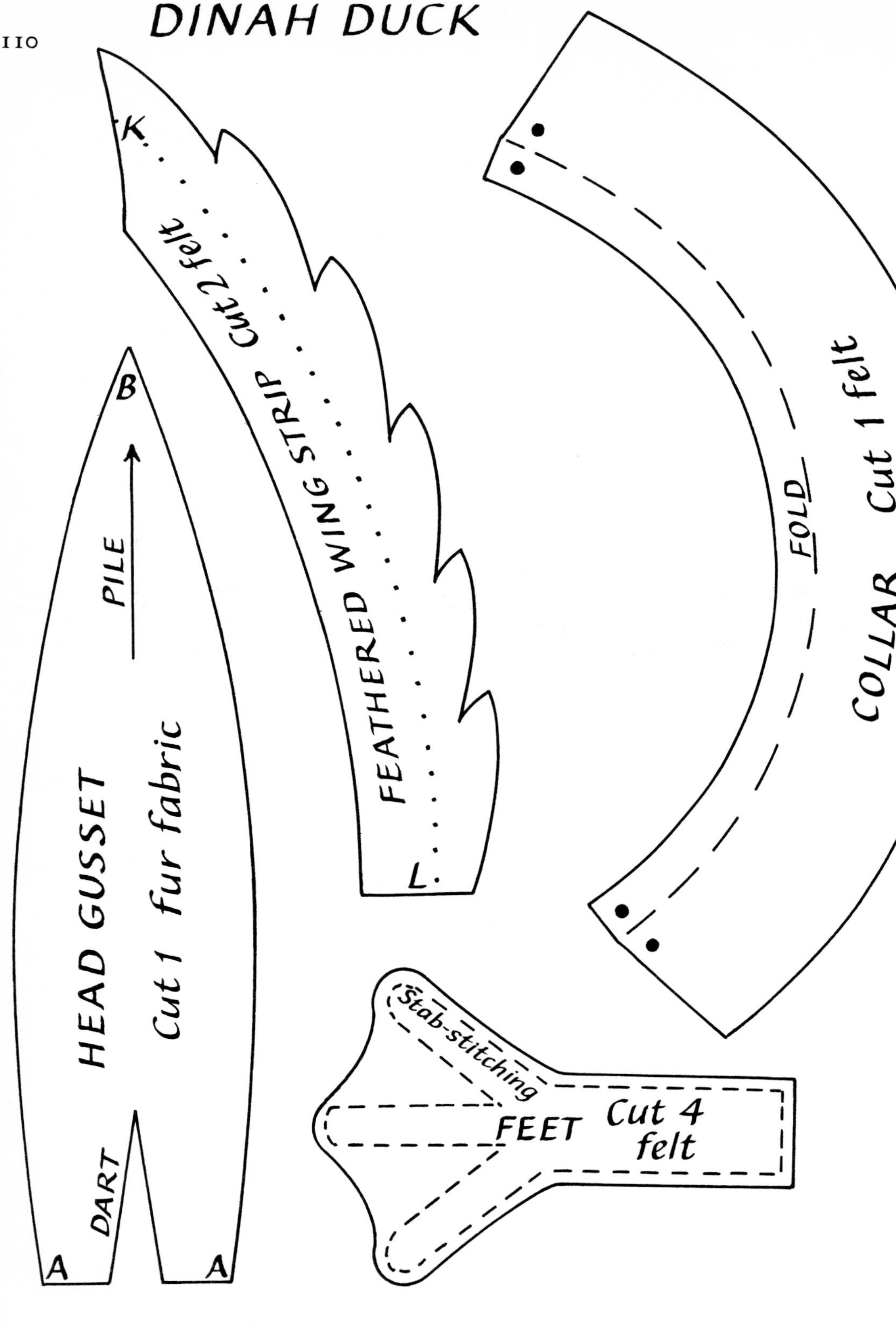

K.

FEATHERED WING STRIP Cut 2 felt

L.

B

PILE

HEAD GUSSET

Cut 1 fur fabric

DART

A   A

FOLD

COLLAR Cut 1 felt

Stab-stitching

FEET Cut 4 felt

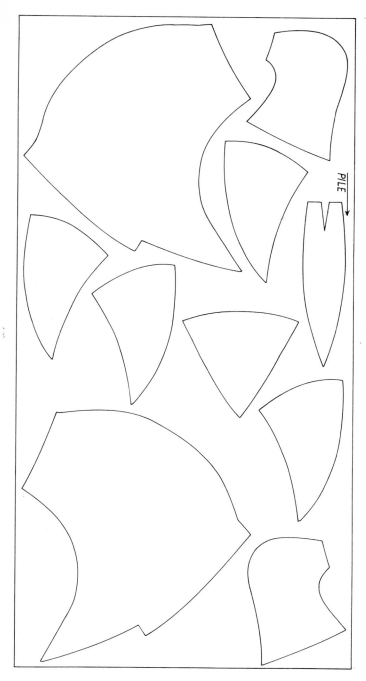

PILE

Dinah Duck: Chart 1
White fur fabric   12″ × 24″

DINAH DUCK

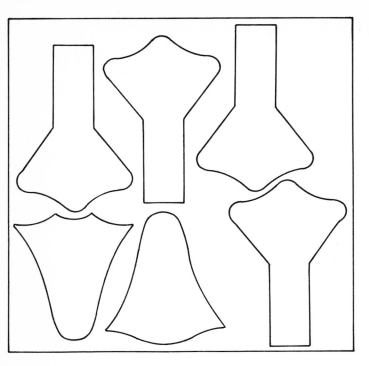

Chart 2: Orange felt 6″ × 6″

Chart 3: White felt 6″ × 5″

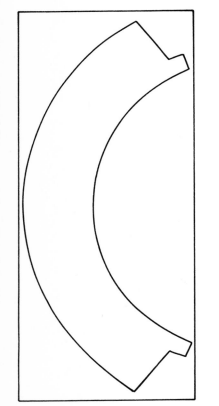

Chart 4: Green felt
7″ × 3″

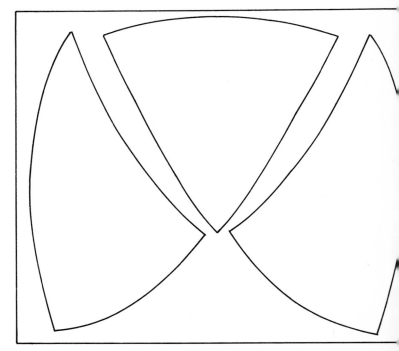

Chart 5: Iron-on Vilene 6″ :

the edge of the felt. The lower edges of the wings are hemmed to the felt 'feather' strips and the base of the body is also hemmed round the opening. Use a strong sewing cotton (see page 10) for all seams.

Tacking. It is advisable to use a self-coloured tacking cotton on the turnings round the base of the head, neck and on the wings, making a long stitch on the inside—about $\frac{1}{2}$ inch—and a very short one on the outside so that the tacking thread can be left in, as the small stitches will not show in the depth of the pile. Use a coloured cotton to mark the positions of the eyes on the outside of the fabric and the leg positions on the base of the body as given on the pattern.

Templates. Trace off the pattern pieces on pages 108–110 and make thin card templates as instructed on page 26. Arrange the pattern pieces for the fur fabric on the back of the material, as arranged in Chart 1, with the pile stroking in the direction of the arrows. Allow a $\frac{1}{2}$ inch space between the pattern pieces for the $\frac{1}{4}$ inch turnings. Place the orange felt sections as shown on Chart 2, the white sections as on Chart 3 and the green collar as on Chart 4. No allowance for turnings is necessary.

The white felt sections requiring Iron-on Vilene for the wings and tail are prepared as explained below and in the paragraph for Iron-on Vilene, page 19. The lay-out is on Chart 5.

Marking and Cutting out (see page 27). Mark out closely round the edges of the templates, using a finely pointed pencil. Mark also the eye, leg and wing positions through the perforations. Cut out the fur fabric allowing $\frac{1}{4}$ inch turnings *beyond* the marking out line and cut the felt without turnings—just inside the marking out line.

IRON-ON VILENE SECTIONS

To prepare the tail and one pair of wings, mark out these sections on the Vilene (smooth side) as given on Chart 5 and cut them out without turnings. Place them within the marking out lines on the back of the fur fabric pieces, the rough side to the back of the fabric, and press well together with a fairly hot iron.

INSERTION OF THE EYES

Using 13 mm. brown eyes, attach them to the positions as marked on the pattern, from the instructions. Method I page 21.

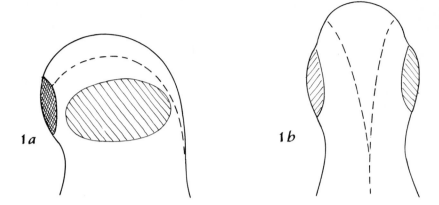

**Back and side views of the extra cushions of stuffing
to shape the sides of the head**

THE HEAD

a. Pin the head gusset to a 'side of head' piece at A and B, and then between at about 1 inch intervals. Back-stitch from A to B. Repeat this to attach the second 'side of head' piece to the other side of the head gusset. Sew from A to B and then on to C.

b. Close the front seam from D to E, but leave the front of the head open at the beak position.

c. Sew the dart together at the front of the head gusset.

d. Fold back the $\frac{1}{4}$ inch turning at the base of the neck and tack (with small stitches on the outside).

e. Turn the head right side out.

f. The head is now stuffed with 'cushions' of rayon and woodwool (see page 29) but before stuffing the neck, add an extra cushion of filling, placing it horizontally across the head below the eye positions, to obtain a more natural shape (Diagram 1a and 1b). Then lightly stuff the neck down to the base.

THE FINGER-STALL

Make this up from the pattern No. 5 on page 36. Make up and attach it as instructed on pages 37–39, completing the stuffing of the neck at the same time.

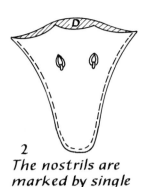

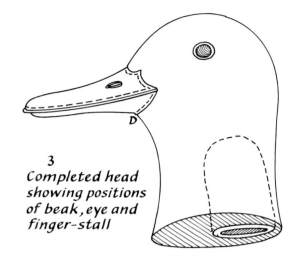

2
*The nostrils are
marked by single
chain stitches*

3
*Completed head
showing positions
of beak, eye and
finger-stall*

THE BEAK

a. Using three strands of stranded cotton in a darker shade than the beak itself, embroider the two nostril marks, each with a single chain stitch (see page 16) on the upper beak where indicated on the pattern and in Diagram 2.

b. Place the upper and lower beak pieces together and stab-stitch finely near the edge along the sides and front, using one thread of cotton in a matching colour.

c. Stuff the beak firmly and evenly, especially the tip.

d. Following Diagram 3 place and pin the beak to the head in a level position over the opening in the head. Add more filling between the beak and the head if needed. Attach the beak to the head with open back-stitching, sewing across the under beak piece first. Open back-stitching will resemble the stab-stitching on the beak and allow more material to be picked up on the needle—making a stronger finish.

THE BODY

First sew in a coloured tacking cotton over the leg position lines at the lower edge of the body. See page 16.

a. Place the two body pieces pile sides together, then pin and sew the front seam E–F and the back seam C–G.

b. Next put the prepared tail piece (see paragraph 'Iron-on Vilene', page 113) to the body and pin G to G and H to H on both sides of the tail and between these points. Back-stitch H G H.

c. Fold up the turnings and form and sew a $\frac{1}{4}$ inch hem across the base of the tail.

d. Similarly, fold under the turnings along the base of the body, but here form and sew a $\frac{1}{2}$ inch hem.

e. Fold in the turnings round the neck opening and tack invisibly, ready to join to the head.

THE WINGS

It is advisable to make the wings as a right and left hand pair at the same time, working each wing as follows:

a. Take a pair of wing pieces, one with Vilene for the front of the wing and one without Vilene for the back. Place the pile sides together and pin first at J and K. Back-stitch this seam.

b. Fold up and tack the $\frac{1}{4}$ inch fur fabric turning between K and L on both pieces with white tacking cotton, making small stitches on the outside (Diagram 4a).

c. To reduce the bulkiness of the turnings of the wing tip at K, cut away the surplus (Diagram 4b). This gives a much neater finish.

d. To the Vilene backed front side of the wing, place and pin the appropriate felt 'feather' strip along the folded edge from K to L as shown in Diagram 4c. Notice that at L the 'feather' strip should end at the marking out line. Allow about $\frac{1}{2}$ inch of the 'feathered' edge to show on the outside beyond the wing, and the remaining $\frac{1}{2}$ inch to overlap behind the wing piece. Pin in place and hem the folded fur fabric edge to the felt strip, K to L.

e. Fold the wing right sides outwards and pin together in the centre to keep the front and back evenly in place (Diagram 4d). Hem the second folded wing edge to the other side of the felt strip to close this part of the wing. Leave the wings open from J to L.

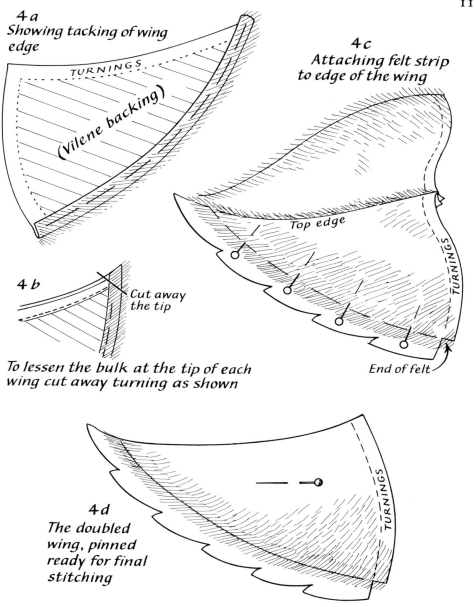

4 a
Showing tacking of wing edge

TURNINGS

(Vilene backing)

4 b
Cut away the tip

To lessen the bulk at the tip of each wing cut away turning as shown

4 c
Attaching felt strip to edge of the wing

Top edge

TURNINGS

End of felt

4 d
The doubled wing, pinned ready for final stitching

TURNINGS

TO ATTACH THE WINGS TO THE BODY

The wings form the sections of the 'glove' used by the thumb and the little finger and are entered through the slits in the body pieces.

    a. Cut the slits marked on each body piece, and then turn the body.

    b. While the body is right side out, insert each wing into its appropriate slit, placing J L to J L. Pin each wing to the body to keep them in place, then turn the body and working on the inside, pin and sew a $\frac{1}{4}$ inch seam round the slit opening, J to L and back to J, with the fur fabric sides together. Do not include the 'feather' edge—this should have ended outside the slit.

    c. Oversew the turnings and then bind the seam round the slit with $\frac{1}{2}$ inch cotton bias binding to prevent any fraying of the raw edges when in use.

SUPPORTS FOR THE LEGS AND FEET

Pipe cleaners are used to form the bone structure of the feet and legs to give them rigidity, being placed between the two felt foot pieces. Each support requires two pipe cleaners and they should be made up by following the progressive illustrated sequence of Diagrams 5a–5k on the opposite page.

    5a and 5b. The first cleaner is shaped to form the outer toes. It is bent in the centre and at approximately 1 inch on either side.

    5c. The ends twisted together to form the leg.

    5d, 5e, 5f. The second pipe cleaner bent in half to become the centre toe and placed over the first pipe cleaner.

    5g. Rayon stuffing (or other suitable material) is wrapped round the leg to fill it out to a circular shape and to make it smooth.

    5h. Adhesive is put on the underside of the foot support, and then it is pressed down on to the felt foot piece.

    5j. Apply a little adhesive on top of the foot support and on the webs between the supports. Place the second felt foot piece over the support and press well together. The sides and webs are then held in place by pins.

    5k. The two pieces of felt are stab-stitched together at the edges and along the bone lines to define the structure.

    5l. Side view of the finished foot and leg.

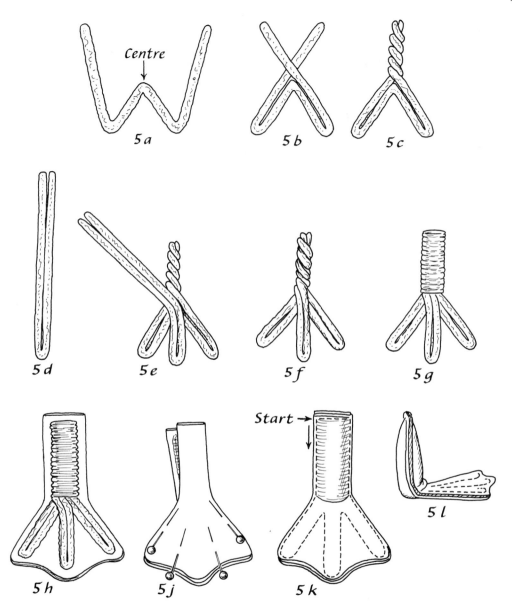

Centre

5 a

5 b

5 c

5 d

5 e

5 f

5 g

5 h

5 j

Start

5 k

5 l

TO ATTACH THE LEGS TO THE BASE OF THE BODY
(Diagrams 6a and 6b)

a. With the body inside out, place the legs in sections P indicated by the dotted lines. Pin in position—the feet level with the edge of the hem, and then oversew the edges of the legs to the back of the fur fabric. Turn the body right side out.

b. Fold section Q round behind each leg and back-stitch the doubled material on the lines R S between the pile of the fur fabric.

THE INSERTION OF THE HEAD INTO THE TOP OF THE BODY

a. Place the front head and body seams together, with the folded neck edge of the body about $\frac{1}{4}$ inch over the base of the head. Pin at the front and back seams first and then between them. To get the best result, test on the hand for position and manipulation by inserting the thumb and fingers required into the wings and head. Re-pin the edges as necessary.

b. Work a double row of ladder-stitch into the fold round the top of the body to attach it to the head.

THE COLLAR

Check and cut the length of the collar as required for the neck size. Fold along the line indicated on the pattern. Punch a hole at each end in the double thickness (Diagram 7). Place it round the neck just above the join and tie together with Russia braid or narrow ribbon in the front.

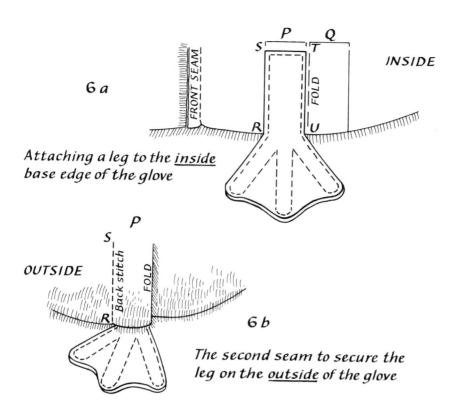

6 a

P   Q

S   T

FRONT SEAM

FOLD

R   U

INSIDE

Attaching a leg to the _inside_
base edge of the glove

P

S

OUTSIDE

Back stitch

FOLD

R

6 b

The second seam to secure the
leg on the _outside_ of the glove

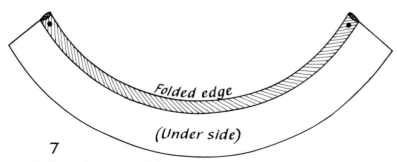

Folded edge

(Under side)

7

Collar showing folded edge with holes through
doubled felt for bow

Henrietta

The natural shape of this design is a good contrast to the other puppets. It is made entirely from felt and the black edging to the 'feather' extremities is a decorative as well as theatrical finish. This hen could of course be made in other poultry colours. A tawny gold body with brown feather edgings would be a very effective choice. The colour of the comb and wattles should be carefully chosen. Light crimson is much more suitable than scarlet. The beak also is an oyster shade—not yellow as so often used. These more subtle shades will repay their selection.

Materials required:

12 in. × 24 in. white felt for the body, head, wings, tail and collar.
6 in. × 9 in. black felt for the 'feather' edging and bow.
3 in. × 6 in. light crimson felt for the comb and wattles.
5 in. × 8 in. oyster felt for the beak and feet.
1 pair brown glass eyes, size 9 mm.
5 pipe cleaners for the feet and leg supports.
Adhesive, U.H.U. or similar.
A thread of six stranded embroidery cotton for the nostrils, and thread of fine sewing cotton or silk for the beak, to match the felt chosen.
4 in. × 3 in. Iron-on Vilene for the back of the tail piece. The stuffing for the head is a mixture of rayon or similar soft filling and foam chippings.

GENERAL INFORMATION

No turnings are needed for felt seams.
Stitching (see also page 13). The seams are sewn on the inside with open back-stitch as near the felt edges as possible—not farther than $\frac{1}{16}$ inch away from it. The top seams of the wings are stab-stitched on the outside as it is best to avoid an inside seam here. The red face patches are hemmed to the

(*Continued on page 130*)

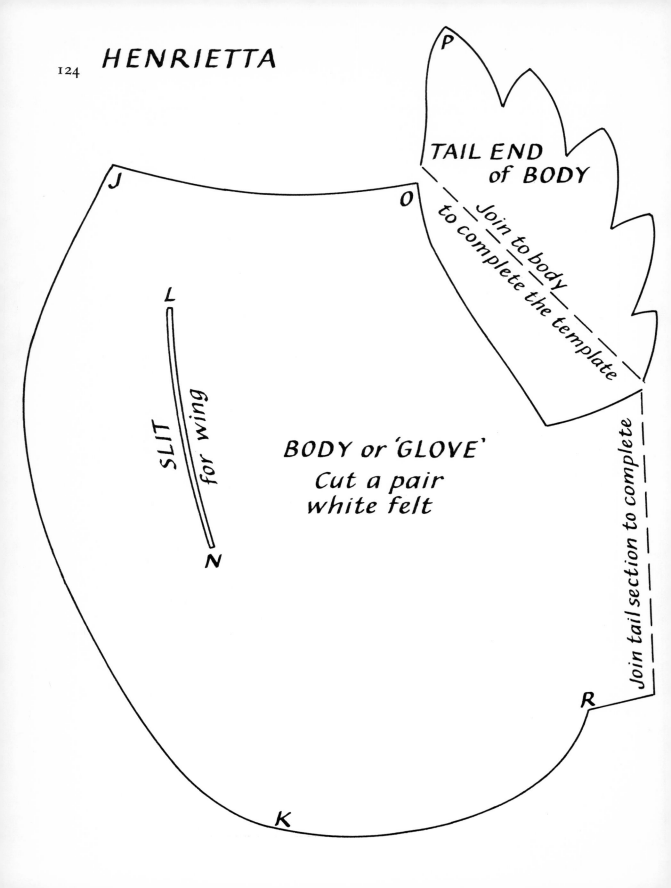

HENRIETTA

TAIL END of BODY

P

J   O

Join to body to complete the template

L

SLIT for wing

N

BODY or 'GLOVE'
Cut a pair white felt

Join tail section to complete

R

K

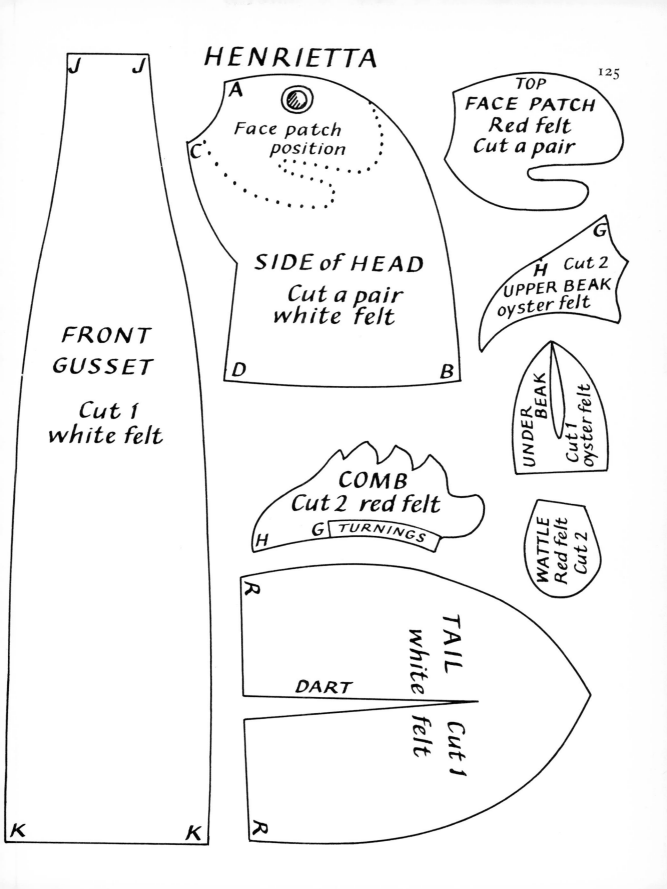

HENRIETTA

125

J J

A

Face patch
position

C

SIDE of HEAD

Cut a pair
white felt

D   B

TOP
FACE PATCH
Red felt
Cut a pair

G

H   Cut 2
UPPER BEAK
oyster felt

UNDER
BEAK

Cut 1
oyster felt

FRONT
GUSSET

Cut 1
white felt

COMB
Cut 2 red felt

H   G TURNINGS

WATTLE
Red felt
Cut 2

R

TAIL
white felt

DART

Cut 1

K   K

R

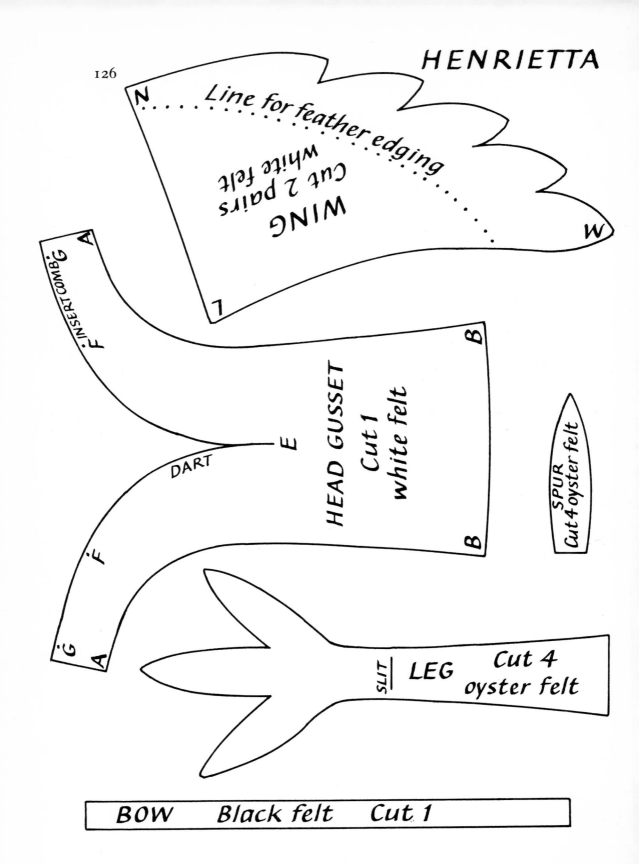

HENRIETTA

N .... Line for feather edging

WING
Cut 2 pairs
white felt

A
G INSERT COMB
F

1

E

DART

F

HEAD GUSSET
Cut 1
white felt

B

B

SPUR
Cut 4 oyster felt

F

G
A

SLIT   LEG   Cut 4
oyster felt

BOW   Black felt   Cut 1

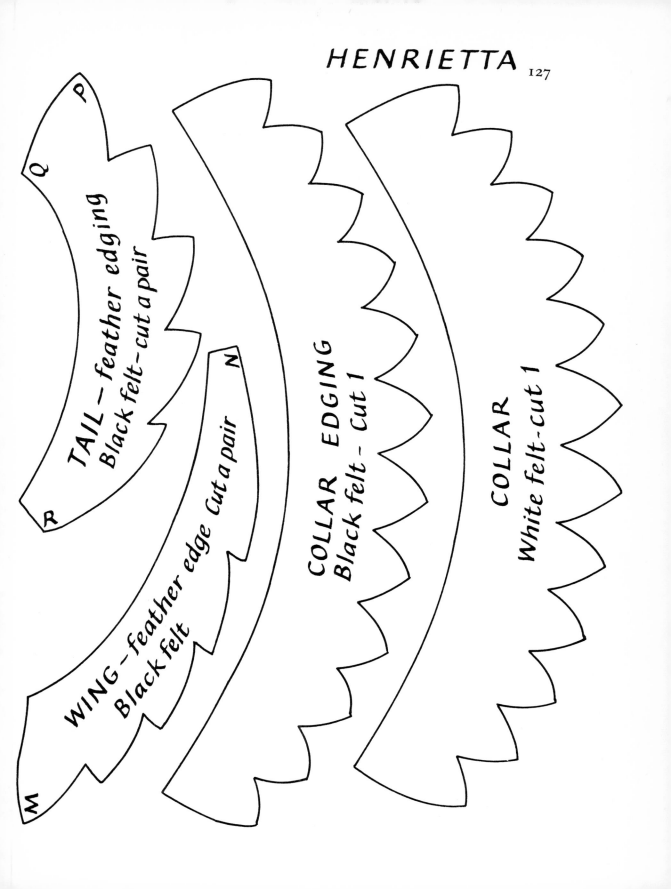

P

Q

R

TAIL – feather edging
Black felt – cut a pair

N

WING – feather edge *Cut a pair*
Black felt

M

COLLAR EDGING
Black felt – Cut 1

COLLAR
White felt – cut 1

Henrietta: Chart 1
White felt   12″ × 24″

Chart 2
Black felt
6" × 9"

Chart 3
Crimson felt
3" × 6"

Chart 4
Oyster felt
5" × 8"

head. To get a fine edge on the beak the pieces are stab-stitched with small stitches in a fine self-coloured thread. All the threads for the seams should be strong. Coloured tacking cotton is needed to mark the slits and the leg positions on the body pieces (see page 16).

The wings are used as finger-stalls for the thumb and little finger and they are inserted in a forward pointing position through the slits on the body. The slits can be moved a little in any direction to suit individual hands.

TEMPLATES

Trace off the pattern pieces on pages 124–127 as instructed on page 26. No. 2 pattern is used for the finger-stall (see page 34).

Next arrange the templates on the white felt pieces for the body, head, wings, tail and collar as shown on Chart 1, the black felt sections as in Chart 2, and the crimson and the oyster as in Chart 3 and Chart 4.

MARKING AND CUTTING OUT

This is fully described on page 27.

After cutting out it is best to put the small pieces in a polythene bag to prevent loss.

MAKE-UP

1. The head

a. First the comb is prepared ready to insert it into the dart on the head gusset. Smear some adhesive on the inner sides of the two comb pieces and press them firmly together, keeping the edges level. Avoid getting any adhesive on the outside or along the cut edges. Any slight unevenness in the fit of the edges can be removed by careful trimming. Sew invisible running stitches round the edges to further secure the two felts together. (See page 17.)

b. To join the head seams place the head pieces to the gusset, 'right' sides together. Pin one side of the head gusset, A B to A B on the appropriate head piece, pinning first at the corners and then between, with the pins at right angles to the edges. Open back-stitch an inside seam from A to B near the edges of the felt. Similarly attach the second side of the head to the gusset.

c. To attach the Section 1 pieces of crimson felt, pin and hem each to the outside of the head so that the top edges just cover the seams A B and the front edges are level with the front of the head (see pattern and Diagram 1).

d. The eyes are inserted next at the position indicated on the patch pattern by Method I given on page 21.

e. Pin and back-stitch the front inside seam C D.

f. Starting at E on the head dart, pin and back-stitch the inside seam as far as F (Diagram 2). Next invert the comb and put the F G section of it into the remainder of the dart (F G). Continue the dart seam to G, which is $\frac{1}{8}$ inch before the corner. The remainder of the comb G H is included in the top of the beak later.

g. Turn the head right side out.

2. *The beak* consists of three pieces of felt, two for the upper and one for the lower beak. To make up the beak each seam is worked from the tip and finely stab-stitched in fine sewing cotton on the outside.

a. The nostril marks on the upper beak pieces are made by working a single chain stitch in the position given on the pattern. (How to work chain

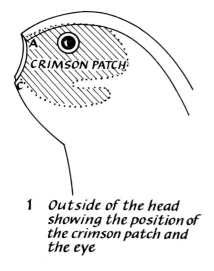

1 *Outside of the head showing the position of the crimson patch and the eye*

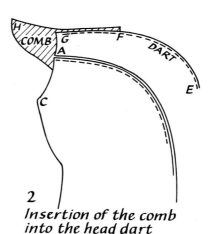

2 *Insertion of the comb into the head dart*

stitch is shown on page 16.) Use three strands of a six-stranded embroidery cotton or four threads of Sylko.

b. Close the centre dart on the lower beak by oversewing an inside seam (Diagram 3a).

c. Next pin and stab-stitch an upper beak to each side of the lower beak. The top seam is sewn last, stab-stitching from the tip of the beak to H (see Diagram 3b). Then place the base of the comb H G (which is projecting from the head seam) between the upper beak pieces and include it in the seam to G. Allow for $\frac{1}{8}$ inch of the beak to be sewn over the edge of the head felt (Diagram 3c).

d. Stuff the beak firmly with rayon or soft filling keeping the tip well pointed.

e. Next attach the beak to the head by overlapping it $\frac{1}{8}$ inch. Pin and open back-stitch the join to resemble the stab-stitching on the other parts of the beak.

f. The crimson wattles are hemmed to the under beak from the end of the dart to the bases of the face patches (see Diagram 3d).

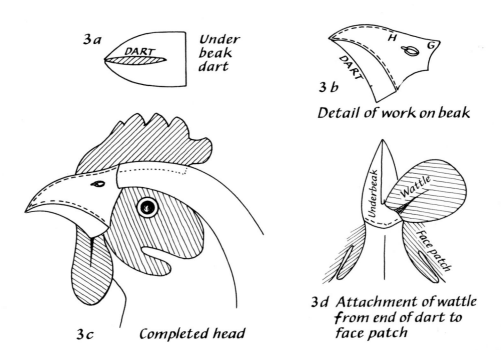

3a   DART   Under beak dart

3b   Detail of work on beak

3c   Completed head

3d Attachment of wattle from end of dart to face patch

g. Stuff the head with rayon and foam chippings evenly mixed and made into cushions of suitable sizes (see page 29). The base of the neck should be lightly stuffed until the finger-stall has been inserted.

3. *The finger-stall*

Make this up from the pattern No. 2 on page 34. Construct and insert it as instructed on pages 37–39, completing the stuffing of the neck at the same time.

4. *The body and wings*

Make up the wings as a pair, each wing having a back and a front section with a black 'feather' strip between them along the base of each wing.

   a. Sew in a coloured tacking cotton to mark the positions of the slits for the wings and the lines for the leg positions on each body piece.
   b. Place and pin the front gusset between the two body pieces, J to J and K to K, and back-stitch the two front inside seams.
   c. On the back section of each wing, fit the 'black feather' strip $\frac{1}{8}$ inch beyond the edges of each 'feather' point of the wing as shown in Diagram 5a. Stick the wing points securely to the black strip. Avoid showing any adhesive at the edges. Attach the curved edge of the black strip to the wing with adhesive and by hemming invisibly along the edge.

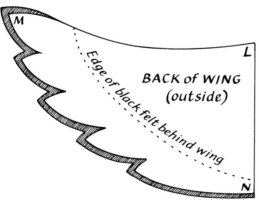

5 a *Back piece of the wing with black feather strip added*

5 b *Wing showing back and front sections placed with black feather strip between the 'feather' edge*

d. The front section of each wing is now added (Diagram 5b) first pinning it to the back section along the top edge, again allowing $\frac{1}{8}$ inch of the black strip to show along the base. Secure the 'feather' points to the black strip with adhesive as above.

e. Remove the pins and hem the inner edge of the black strip to the inside of the front of the wing, in the thickness only of the white felt.

f. A stitch with white thread between the base of each feather will more securely attach the two felts on both the back and front sections of the wings.

g. Finally stab-stitch together the top edges of each wing as an outside seam from L to M. Do not close the openings to the wings at the straight edge (L–N).

5. *To attach the wings to the body*

Check that the slits are cut to the same length as L N on the wings.

a. Place and pin each wing in position on the outside of the body piece— the open ends level with the slits.

b. On the inside, pin the back and front edges of the open ends of the wings L N to the sides of the slits to form access into the wings. Back-stitch the wing openings to the slits about $\frac{1}{16}$ inch from the edges

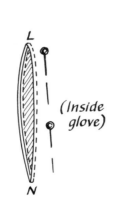

6   *Wing inserted and stitched to the slit*

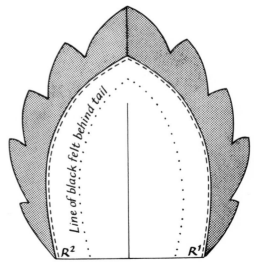

7   *Back view of the tail*

(Diagram 6) and then oversew the felt edges to resist wear and tear in use.

c. Complete the body seams by closing the back as an inside seam O P.

d. Turn the body right side out.

6. *The Tail*

a. To attach the 'feather' strip to the tail, first join the two black 'feather' strips together from P to Q as shown on the pattern.

b. Place and pin the strips behind the feathered edge on the tail of the body pieces allowing the black 'feather' edge to show $\frac{1}{8}$ inch beyond the white 'feather' edge. Attach with adhesive and invisible sewing as on the wings (Diagram 5a). Hem the inner edge of the strip to the body (in the thickness of the felt).

c. To support the tail in an erect position on the wrist, the tail piece is reinforced with Iron-on Vilene (see page 19). This is now ironed on to the inside of the tail piece.

d. Pin and back-stitch the dart and treat it as an inside seam.

e. Place and pin the tail piece in position behind the black strips. Pin R to R first at the base corners and then pin at the top of the tail piece. (The edge of the tail piece should cover about $\frac{1}{2}$ inch of the straight edge of the black strip as shown in Diagram 7 from R^1 to R^2. Finally back-stitch along the edge through the felts without showing stitches on the body side.

7. *The legs and feet*

a. Diagram 8a shows the general construction for each leg. Pipe cleaners each 6 inches long are used as stiffeners. Fold each cleaner as shown in 8a and b. Use 8a as the centre toe and leg and 8b, bent into a V shape, for the outer 'toes'.

b. Wrap each doubled pipe cleaner with a thin length of rayon stuffing, tapering each 'toe' to a point. Wind cotton thread over this to keep it in place. Put 8b on top of 8a at the position to form the shape of the foot pattern and secure them together (8c).

c. Place together two felt leg and foot pieces and stab-stitch very near the edge from the top of the leg round the toes to X (8d).

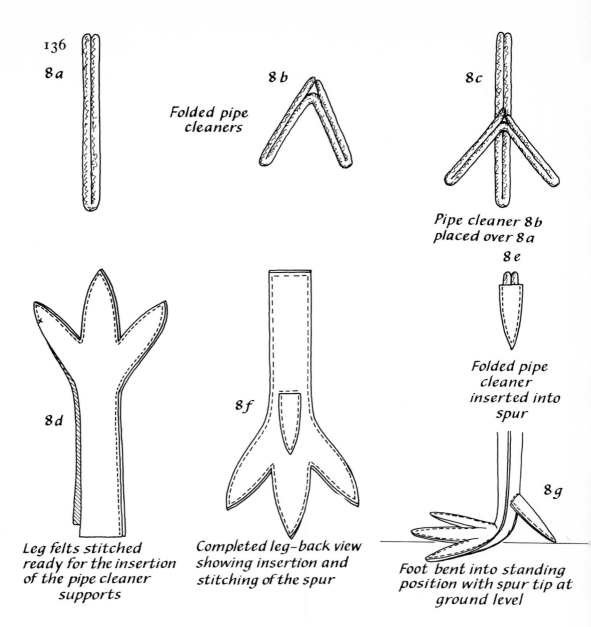

136

8a

8b

*Folded pipe
cleaners*

8c

*Pipe cleaner 8b
placed over 8a*

8e

*Folded pipe
cleaner
inserted into
spur*

8d

*Leg felts stitched
ready for the insertion
of the pipe cleaner
supports*

8f

*Completed leg–back view
showing insertion and
stitching of the spur*

8g

*Foot bent into standing
position with spur tip at
ground level*

   d. Insert the pipe cleaner framework into the toes and leg and pin in
position. Continue the stab-stitching to the top of the leg adding
filling as required. Stab-stitch across the top to close the leg.

   e. To make the 'toe' at the back of the leg, stab-stitch together the sides of
the two pieces of felt for the toe leaving the straight end open. Insert a
$2\frac{1}{2}$ inch piece of pipe cleaner doubled, wrapped and bound as for the
front toes (8e).

f. Cut the $\frac{1}{4}$ inch slit across the back of the leg as marked on the pattern and shown in Diagram 8f. With the aid of a stiff needle insert the toe at least $\frac{1}{4}$ inch into the slit and up the leg. Secure it by back-stitching across the slit and then ladder-stitch the under side of the toe to the leg. Bend the foot to a standing position so that the tip of the back toe reaches the ground level (Diagram 8g).

8. Attaching the body to the head

Place the neck edge of the body just above the stitching round the base of the head centralizing the front and back of the head to the body. Pin in between to keep the overlap of the two parts at about $\frac{1}{8}$ inch. Back-stitch round the neck along this overlap to secure the body to the head as shown in Diagram 9a.

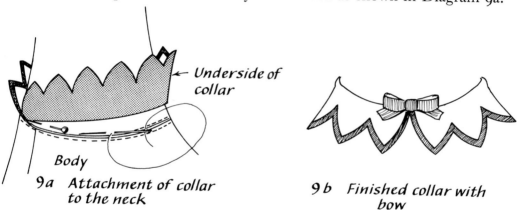

9a Attachment of collar to the neck

9b Finished collar with bow

9. The collar

Place the black 'feather' edging under the collar piece so that $\frac{1}{8}$ inch shows beyond it forming a black edge. Apply adhesive to stick the 'feather' points together and hem the straight inner edge of the black strip invisibly to the collar as in the make up of the wings.

Place and pin the collar round the neck in an inverted position (Diagram 9a) and back-stitch the edge to the neck. Turn down the collar, and make the narrow strip of black felt into a bow, stitch it in place slightly above the collar (Diagram 9b).

10. Attaching the legs to the body

Pin the legs in position at K, given on the pattern at the base of the glove, leaving approximately 1 inch of leg showing below the edge of the glove, or half the leg inside and half below. This can be adjusted to individual requirements. Stitch it to the inside securely but without it being visible on the outside.

Chekko, the Clown

A clown is always a fascinating and attractive addition to any group of puppets, as well as an endearing personality when used alone. The felt appliqué method of producing the face is a useful exercise for many other faces for both puppets and dolls. As a useful alternative, patterns are given for a pair of boxing gloves as well as the traditional white gloves.

The materials required are:

9 in. × 22 in. flesh pink felt for the head, legs, feet and finger-stall.

5 in. × 8 in. scarlet felt for the features and shoe uppers.

10 in. × 12 in. white felt for the mouth, hat, gloves, etc.

2 in. × 8 in. black felt for the shoe soles and eyebrows and nostrils.

8 in. × 6 in. brown or black felt or gloving leather for the pair of boxing gloves (if made instead of white gloves).

Small pieces of felt—pale blue and royal blue—for the eyes.

3 in. × 27¼ in. tarlatan or similar white material for the ruff.

A strip of gold mohair fur fabric for hair—2½ inches wide and 13 inches long (the stroke of the pile across the width).

¼ yard of coloured ribbon, 1¼ inches wide for the hat.

1 card of white bias binding (mercerised).

8 inches long × 24 inches wide coloured cotton with small gay design for the tunic.

10 inches long × 18 inches wide striped or plain material for the trousers.

6 pipe cleaners for the white gloves.

2 pieces white tape, 9 in. long, ⅛ in. wide for the boxing glove ties.

½ yard of narrow ribbon or Russia braid for the ruff.

1 black and 1 white thread of six-stranded embroidery cotton.

A small piece of Iron-on Vilene for the ears.

Stuffing—a mixture of rayon or similar soft filling and foam chippings.

A tube of U.H.U. or similar colourless adhesive.

(Continued on page 150)

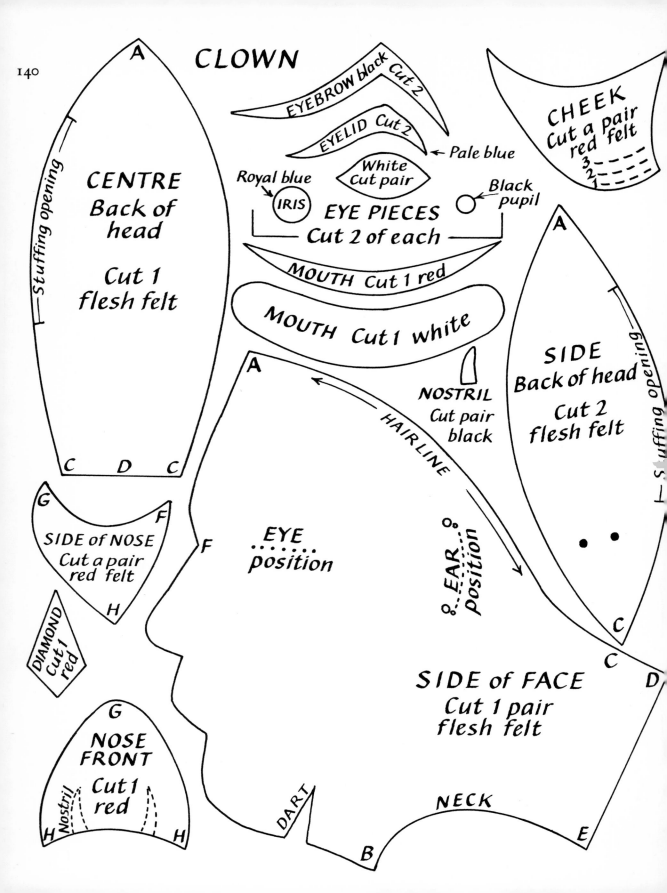

140

CLOWN

CENTRE
Back of
head

Cut 1
flesh felt

Stuffing opening

A

C D C

EYEBROW black Cut 2

EYELID Cut 2

← Pale blue

White
Cut pair

Royal blue

IRIS

EYE PIECES
Cut 2 of each

Black
pupil

MOUTH Cut 1 red

MOUTH Cut 1 white

NOSTRIL
Cut pair
black

CHEEK
Cut a pair
red felt

3
2
1

A

SIDE
Back of head

Cut 2
flesh felt

Stuffing opening

A

HAIRLINE

EYE
position

EAR
Position

C

C

G

F

SIDE of NOSE
Cut a pair
red felt

F

H

DIAMOND
Cut 1
red

G

NOSE
FRONT

Cut 1
red

Nostril

H H

DART

B

SIDE of FACE
Cut 1 pair
flesh felt

D

NECK

E

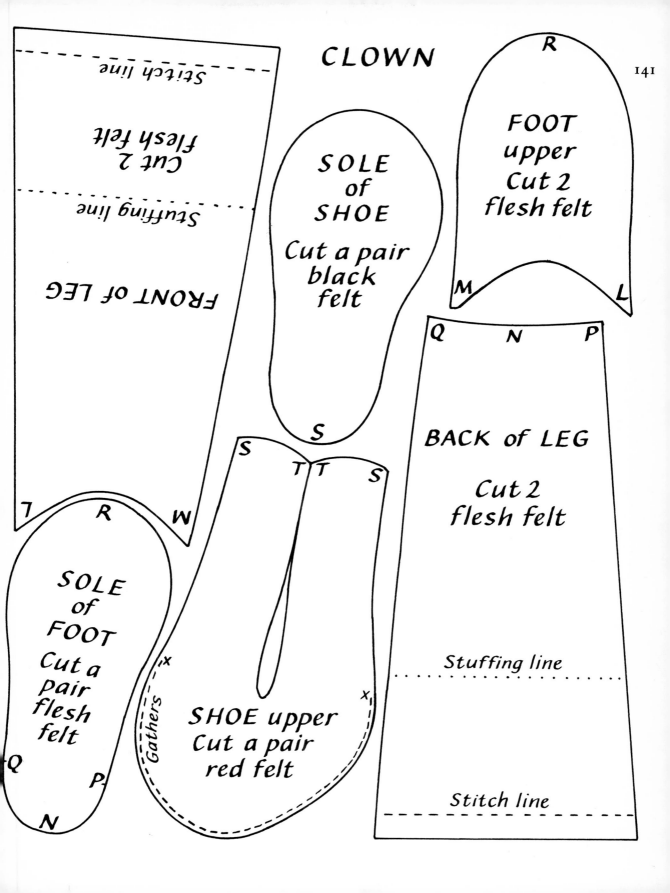

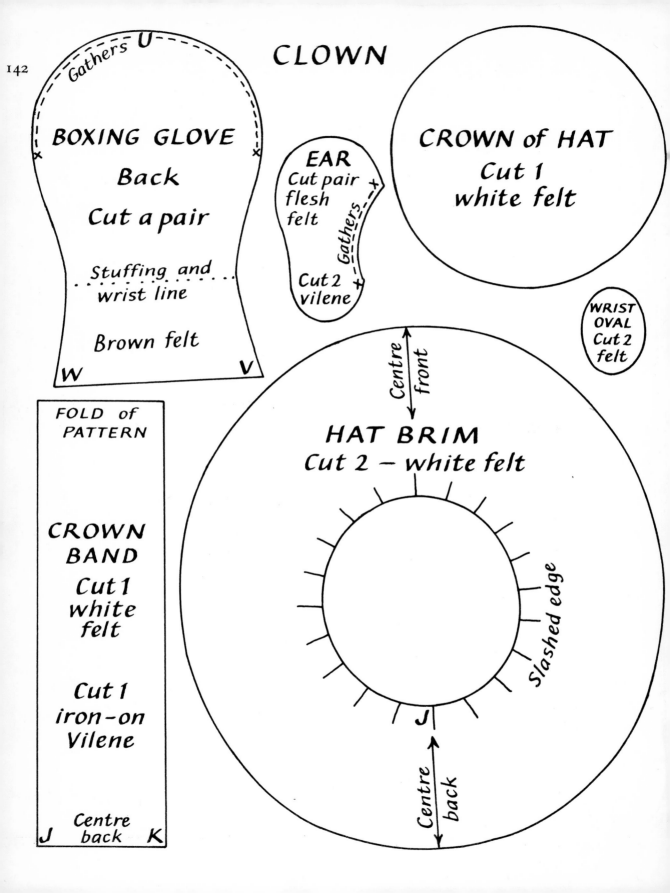

CLOWN

142

Gathers U

BOXING GLOVE
Back
Cut a pair

Stuffing and
wrist line

Brown felt

W   V

EAR
Cut pair
flesh
felt

Cut 2
vilene

Gathers

CROWN of HAT
Cut 1
white felt

WRIST
OVAL
Cut 2
felt

FOLD of
PATTERN

CROWN
BAND

Cut 1
white
felt

Cut 1
iron-on
Vilene

Centre
back

J   K

Centre front

HAT BRIM
Cut 2 — white felt

Slashed edge

J

Centre back

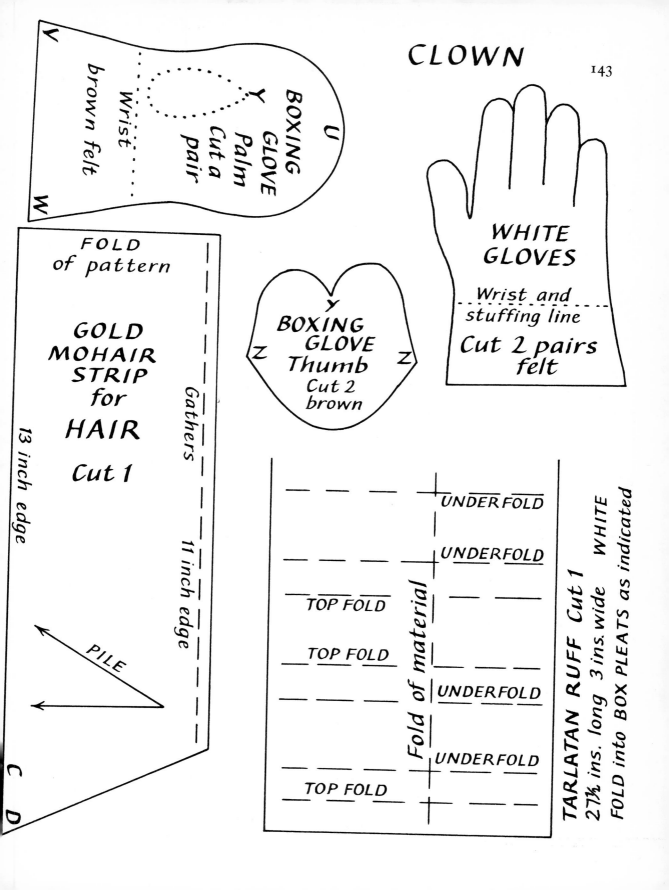

BOXING GLOVE Palm
Y
Cut a pair

V — W
Wrist
brown felt
U

WHITE GLOVES

Wrist and stuffing line

Cut 2 pairs felt

FOLD of pattern

GOLD MOHAIR STRIP for HAIR

Cut 1

Gathers

11 inch edge

13 inch edge

PILE

C — D

BOXING GLOVE Thumb
y
N — Z
Cut 2 brown

UNDERFOLD

UNDERFOLD

TOP FOLD

TOP FOLD

Fold of material

UNDERFOLD

UNDERFOLD

TOP FOLD

TARLATAN RUFF Cut 1
27½ ins. long 3 ins. wide WHITE
FOLD into BOX PLEATS as indicated

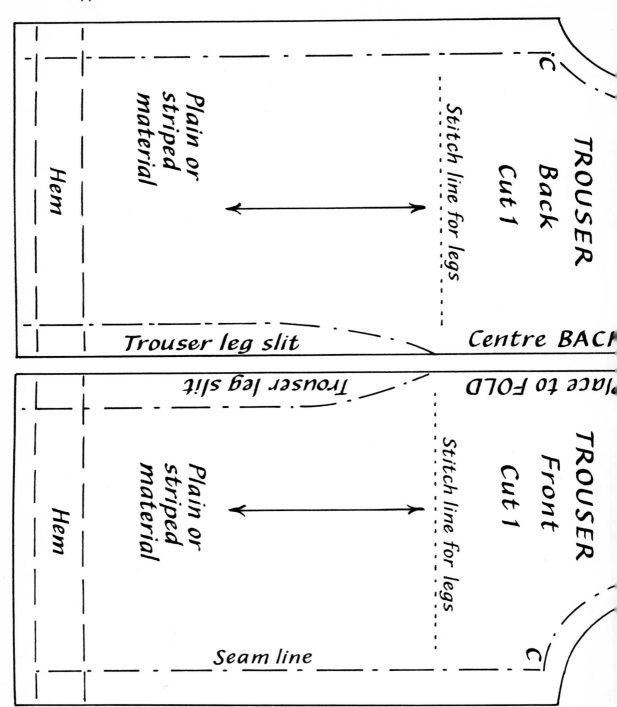

TROUSER
Back
Cut 1

Stitch line for legs

Plain or striped material

Hem

Trouser leg slit

Centre BACK

Place to FOLD

Trouser leg slit

TROUSER
Front
Cut 1

Stitch line for legs

Plain or striped material

Hem

Seam line

CLOWN

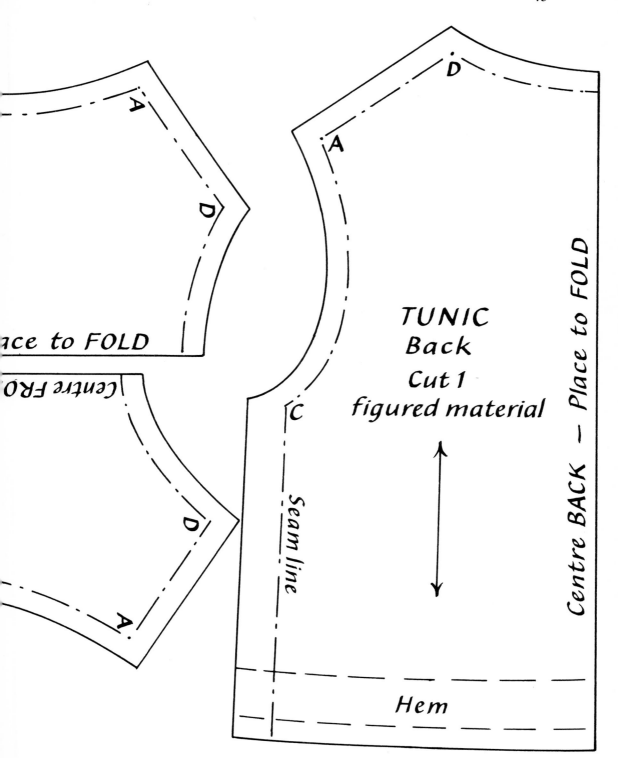

A

D

Place to FOLD

Centre FRONT

D

A

D

A

C

TUNIC
Back
Cut 1
figured material

Seam line

Hem

Centre BACK — Place to FOLD

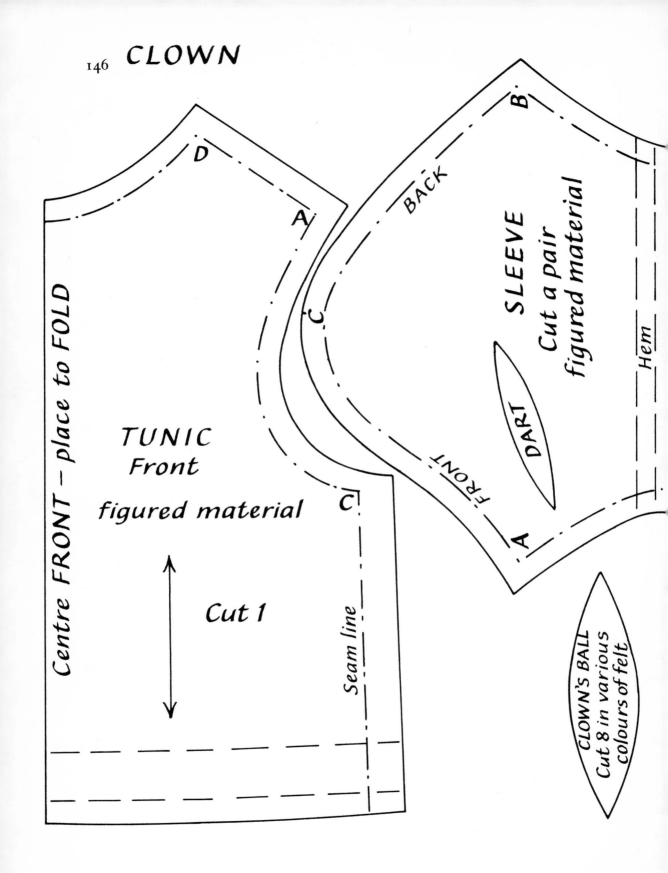

D

A

BACK

B

SLEEVE
Cut a pair
figured material

C

Centre FRONT – place to FOLD

TUNIC
Front

figured material

Cut 1

Seam line

FRONT

C

A

DART

Hem

CLOWN'S BALL
Cut 8 in various
colours of felt

Chart 1   Scarlet felt $5'' \times 8''$

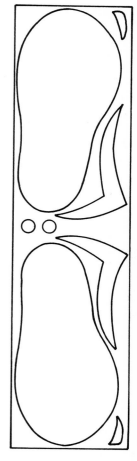

Chart 2
Black felt
$2'' \times 8''$

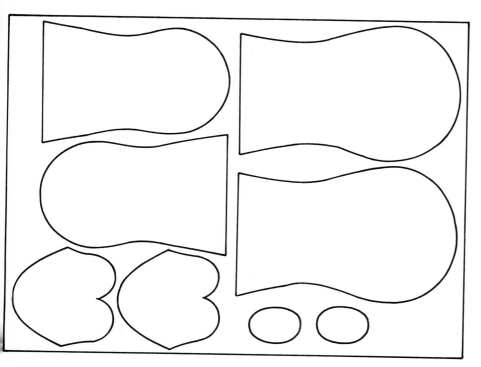

Chart 3   Brown felt $8'' \times 6''$

Chart 4
Light blue
felt
$1'' \times 2''$

Chart 5
Royal blue
felt
$1'' \times 1''$

CLOWN

Chart 6   White felt   10″ × 12″

Chart 7   Flesh pink felt   9″ × 22″

GENERAL INFORMATION

Turnings are not generally necessary on felt but where they are required indication is given on the pattern piece concerned.

Stitching. The inside seams for the felt head, leg, shoes and boxing gloves are open back-stitched with a strong sewing thread, near the edge (see page 13).

It is advisable to pin the work stage by stage as it progresses and seams should be pinned first at each end and then between as required, at right angles to the edges.

The features are made up first. They are attached to the outside of the head by adhesive. Invisible running stitches in the thickness of the felt should also be used to secure the edges of the features to the face. A fine thread such as Machine Embroidery cotton, No. 50 or sewing silk should be used for this purpose (see page 17).

The costume can be hand sewn or machined where suitable. Information on stitches is given on page 13.

Templates. With the exception of the tunic and trousers patterns which are cut in greaseproof paper, trace off the pattern pieces on pages 140–146, and make thin card template as instructed on page 26. Size no. 1 on page 34 is suggested for the finger-stall of this puppet.

Marking out. Arrange the pattern pieces on the felts as shown by each appropriate chart, pages 147–149. Mark out on the back of the felts, along the edges of the templates with a well sharpened tailor's chalk or a finely pointed pencil. A fine marking-out line is essential. Except on black it is easier and better to mark out the small pieces with a pencil.

Cutting out (see also page 27). With sharp scissors cut out the felt pieces just inside the marking-out lines. Make sure that the small pieces of felt are accurate. Check each piece with its template after cutting out, as any deviation in size can alter or spoil the final expression of the face, etc. Small sharp scissors are useful for cutting out the features, and it is advisable to put the cut out pieces in a small polythene bag to avoid loss.

Iron-on Vilene. It is recommended as a slight stiffener for the Clown's ears— and can be used on the back of other pieces, such as the head, should the felt be of a thin poor quality. Similarly it can be applied to thin cotton material if used for the tunic. Refer to page 19.

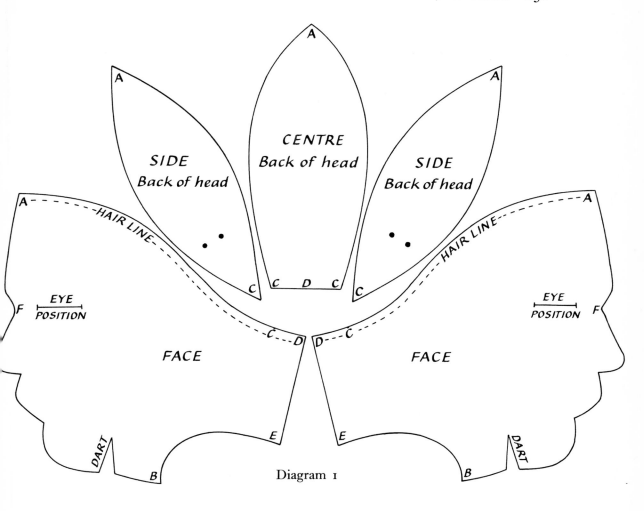

Diagram 1

MAKE-UP OF THE HEAD

1. *FOUNDATION* (*Diagram 1 shows the lay-out of the pattern pieces*)

a. Pin and finely back-stitch the two chin darts on the inside of the material.

b. Place the 'side of face' pieces right sides together. Pin and back-stitch from A to B as an inside seam down the centre front from the forehead to the neck.

c. To make up the back of the head, place the appropriate side pieces to

2 *Face showing positions of all
attached features, ruff and hat*

the centre 'back of head' piece, A C to A C. Pin and sew the two inside seams, except at the stuffing opening.

d. Place the made up 'back of the head' to the 'side of face' pieces and pin and sew the seams A C to A C along the 'hair line' on each side of the face. Then pin and sew the two short seams C D and the back of the neck seam D E. This completes the foundation of the head, on which, after stuffing, the features are applied.

e. Turn the head right side out.

2. STUFFING THE HEAD

As the 'cushion' method of stuffing will help to form and support the contours of the face, detailed directions are given (see also page 29).

Firm cushions of rayon filling and foam chippings evenly mixed are made in various shapes and sizes which, as the work proceeds, are kept in place temporarily with one or two short hat pins passed through the head. Stuff through the stuffing opening after protecting the felt with folded cotton tape tacked over the edges.

First make a cushion to fill the top of the head, then proceed down the face. The forehead cushion should be long enough to reach across the eyebrows, giving them sufficient prominence. Make a triangular cushion for the nose and a round one for the chin, each of a size to fit firmly into the cavities. Keep each new cushion in place with a short hat pin. Next fill the cheeks with one large cushion in each and then add cushions to fill the back of the head and more filling as necessary between them to fill the gaps. The lower part should be lightly filled until the finger-stall is inserted. Remove the hat pins.

3. THE FINGER-STALL

Make this up from the pattern No. 1 on page 34. Insert and attach it as instructed on page 37, completing the stuffing of the neck at the same time. Remove the tape and close the stuffing opening at the back of the head, with ladder-stitching, adding more filling if required.

4. THE FEATURES

Detailed instructions for all the features and the make-up of the face are given so that the best expression can be obtained in this rather unusual method of applied felt work.

First make up the various features and place and pin them in position on the face so as to be able to make adjustments if necessary before they are secured. Refer to Diagram 2 for the positions.

a. *The eye positions*. The shape of the face is greatly improved if the eyebrows are given more than natural prominence. To do this, depressions are formed by means of bracing stitches across the eye positions (over which the eyes are later placed).

This method is shown in Diagram 3a. Using a long needle and a separate thread for each eye, insert the needle at one of the two large

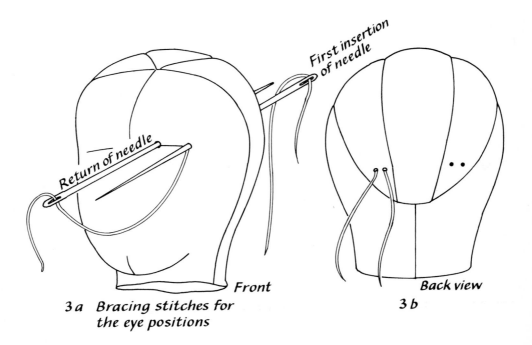

3a **Bracing stitches for the eye positions**

3b

spots marked on the left at the back of the head and pass it through the head to come out at one end of the left eye position line. Insert it at the other end of this line and push it through the head to come out at the second spot ($\frac{1}{4}$ inch from where it was first put in at the back of the head). Leave both ends of the threads hanging free (Diagram 3b). Repeat with another thread for the right eye position. Next make the eye depressions by pressing back from the front while pulling up each pair of thread ends very tightly at the back of the head and tying them securely.

b. *The eyes* (Diagrams 4a–f). The three pieces of felt which form each eye are shown at Diagram 4a.

They are assembled as follows:

With a small amount of adhesive, stick the pupil to the centre of the royal blue iris (Diagram 4b) and secure it with invisible stitches as explained on page 17.

Work a small triangular highlight in satin-stitch—the same size on each pupil with one thread of white stranded embroidery cotton (Diagram 4c).

Next stick the iris and pupil to the white eye piece as in Diagram 4d and invisibly stitch them together.

Notice in Diagram 4e the position of the bottom edge of the eyelid and place the lids—as a pair—to just cut across the top of the iris. Insert a

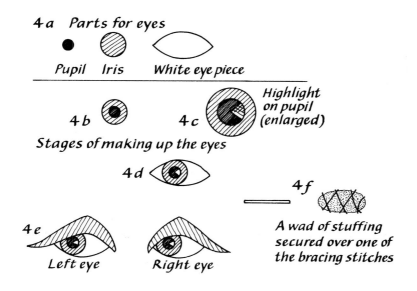

4a   Parts for eyes

Pupil   Iris   White eye piece

4b   4c   Highlight on pupil (enlarged)

Stages of making up the eyes

4d

4f

4e   Left eye   Right eye   A wad of stuffing secured over one of the bracing stitches needle or pin into a tube of adhesive and wipe it along under the lower edge of the eyelid. Press well together as this edge is best left unstitched. On the back of the eye, hem the edge of the lid to the eye in the thickness of the felt only. To give a slightly rounded finish to the eyes, fold up two small wads of soft stuffing—not larger than the white eye felt— and with a little adhesive, stick them over the two bracing stitches on the face. Stitch across each to keep the filling well within the size of the white eyepiece (Diagram 4f). Pin the pair of eyes over the wads of stuffing, placing the inner corners of the eyes at the end of the bracing stitches. This should leave 1 inch between the eyes. The eyes are secured to the face later when all the other features are in place.

c. *The mouth.* First smear a little adhesive on the back of the red felt mouthpiece and place it on the white felt mouth piece, in a central position. Press the edges firmly together. With one thread of black stranded embroidery cotton, back-stitch the centre line through both felts leaving $\frac{3}{8}$ inch unstitched at each end of the mouth as shown in Diagram 2. Pin the mouth to the face as shown in the same diagram and leave it to be sewn on later.

d. *The cheeks* (Diagrams 5a–c). Make up the cheeks as a pair. Sew in the three separate gathering threads which form the three rolls of felt to represent wrinkles on each cheek (Diagram 5a). Follow the marks on

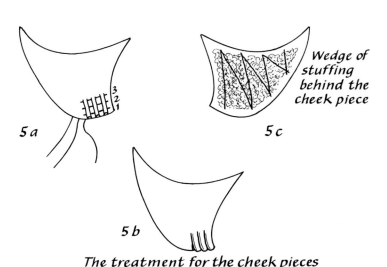

The treatment for the cheek pieces

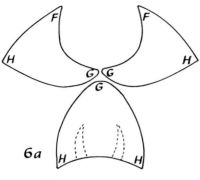

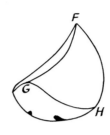

6a   6b

The nose sections   Completed
                                       nose

this diagram and on the pattern exactly. Start stitching in the lower corner of the cheek pieces and work the rows in numerical order. Pull up each row fairly tightly to create the creases for a genial expression, and secure the ends of the threads (Diagram 5b). A wedge of stuffing behind each cheek will round the contours effectively. Place the thickest part towards the wrinkles, and let it taper off on the other side (Diagram 5c). A few long stitches across the wedges of stuffing will keep them in place behind the cheeks or they can be held by pins from the front, until the cheeks are secured. Place and pin the cheeks in position on the face as shown in Diagram 2.

e. *The nose* (Diagrams 6a and b). The three pieces required are shown in position in Diagram 6a and the finished nose at Diagram 6b. The seams are back-stitched on the inside. Pin and sew the upper nose pieces together, F G and then attach the lower nose piece, placing G to G exactly. Sew H–G–H. Make a cushion of stuffing sufficient to fill the nose and place it behind it. Put the stuffed nose in position in the centre of the face. The highest point of the nose at F should be level with the inner corners of the eyes. See Diagram 2. Pin ready to sew later.

f. *The eyebrows, etc.* (see Diagram 7). Place and pin the pair of eyebrows $\frac{1}{2}$ inch above the eyes, with 1 inch between them. Pin the red diamond piece between the eyebrows centrally over the face seam. The lowest point should be level with the ends of the eyebrows.

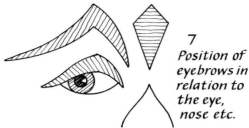

7
Position of eyebrows in relation to the eye, nose etc.

g. *Attaching the features.* First refer to Diagram 2 and check the positions of all the features. Be satisfied that the best possible result has been achieved with a really cheerful expression. Before sewing each feature to the face, apply adhesive evenly to the under side, right out to the edges and then press it well to its position on the face, any excess of adhesive can be pushed back with a needle. With sewing silk, Trylko or Machine Embroidery cotton No. 50, in the same shade as the felt concerned, secure each feature to the face with invisible running stitches near the edges.

It is advisable to attach the features at the top of the face first and work downwards but to facilitate this way of working, remove the nose after marking its position and replace it when all the other features have been secured.

h. *The ears.* It is recommended that the pair of ears are backed with Iron-on Vilene to stiffen the felt, see page 19. Sew in a gathering thread between x . . . x very near the edge of the felt on each ear. Pull up the gathers to wrinkle the ear effectively. Pin the ears in position and attach them to the head by back-stitching over the gathers.

5. THE HAIR

Gold mohair is used for hair and should be cut with the pile in the direction shown on the pattern to allow it to stroke towards the face (see Diagram 2).

a. First fold back a ¼ inch turning along the 13-inch edge, and with small tacking stitches secure this turning to the back of the strip, to keep it in place.

b. Keeping the pile side up and starting at the centre back at D, place and pin the folded edge to the head following the seam D C A C D (called the hair line on the face pattern).
c. Ladder-stitch the folded edge of the strip to the face side of the head seam, to cover the latter.
d. Shorten the end of the strip if it is too long and join it together at the back as an inside seam.
e. Sew in a gathering thread along the 11-inch edge and pull it up to fit the mohair closely to the head. Secure the thread. The bare centre will be covered with the hat which will be stitched on later.

6. THE HAT (Diagram 8a–c)

The Clown's hat consists of the brim, crown circle and crown band. The brim is made of two pieces of felt stuck together to stiffen and strengthen it. The crown seams are back-stitched on the inside of the hat.

Make up the hat as follows:

a. Place the two pieces for the brim, centre backs and centre fronts together. Apply adhesive evenly over the inner surface of one piece and stick the other firmly to it.
b. The crown. Starting at J pin and sew one long edge of the band to the circle (Diagram 8a). If necessary shorten the band to meet and fit at J. Stitch the seam J–K across the band.

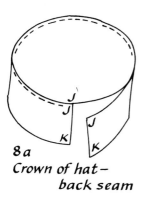

8a
Crown of hat –
    back seam

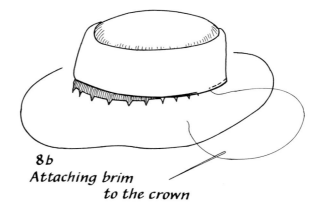

8b
Attaching brim
    to the crown

8c Completed hat

    c. Cut the $\frac{1}{4}$ inch slashes on the inner edge of the brim as marked on the pattern.

    d. Place and pin the crown band over the slashed $\frac{1}{4}$ inch turnings and back-stitch the band to the turnings on the outside of the hat keeping J to J at the back (Diagram 8b).

    e. Fill the hat with a soft stuffing and sink the edge of the circle below the top of the crown band (Diagram 8c).

    f. Make and attach the bow of ribbon to the side front of the hat.

    g. Place the hat on the head at a jaunty angle with the crown band seam at the back. Leave about 1 inch of hair to show under it, and pin in position.

    h. Ladder-stitch the hat to the head, along the *underside* of the hat. Be sure that the hat entirely covers the bare centre of the head.

7. *THE LEGS AND FEET* (Diagram 9)

These are made up in flesh pink felt with open back-stitched inside seams. Make up each as follows:

    a. Pin and sew the upper foot to the base of the 'front of leg' piece L to M.

    b. Pin the sole at N to N at the centre base of the 'back of leg' piece, then pin P to P and Q to Q and stitch P N Q as an inside seam.

    c. To join the upper foot to the sole, pin them together first at R and then at the junction of the seams L M with P Q. Stitch the inside seam round the foot to close it. Continue up the side of the leg to the top. Then stitch the second leg seam to the top to complete the leg, and turn it right side out. Make up the second leg in the same way.

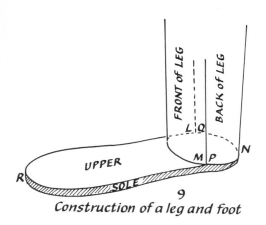

9
Construction of a leg and foot

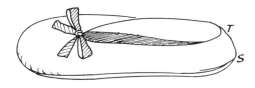

10 *Completed shoe*

d. Stuff the feet and legs to the stuffing line, then back-stitch across the leg along the stuffing line to enclose the filling. By stuffing up to this line only, it allows the Clown to be held in a sitting, as well as standing position.

e. The legs are attached to the trousers later when the costume is made up.

8. THE SHOES (Diagram 10)

Each is made up with inside seams in the following way:

a. On the upper, stitch the back seam S T and then finely sew in the gathering thread near the edge of the felt between x . . . x.

b. To attach the upper to the sole, work on the inside of the shoe, with the sole uppermost. Pin and stitch from S to the gathers on both sides of the shoe. Pin the centre front of the upper and the sole together. Adjust the gathers to fit the upper to the sole evenly. Complete the seam round the front of the shoe, back-stitching over the gathers.

c. Turn the shoe right side out and fit it on the appropriate foot. A small amount of filling will be needed in the heel to keep its shape. Back-stitch a short seam across the top of the heel to attach the shoe to the foot.

d. Cut a 6 inch length of white felt $\frac{1}{4}$ inch wide. Tie it into a bow and sew to the front of the shoe, at the same time stitching the shoe to the foot under the bow to secure the front of the shoe.

e. Make up the second shoe.

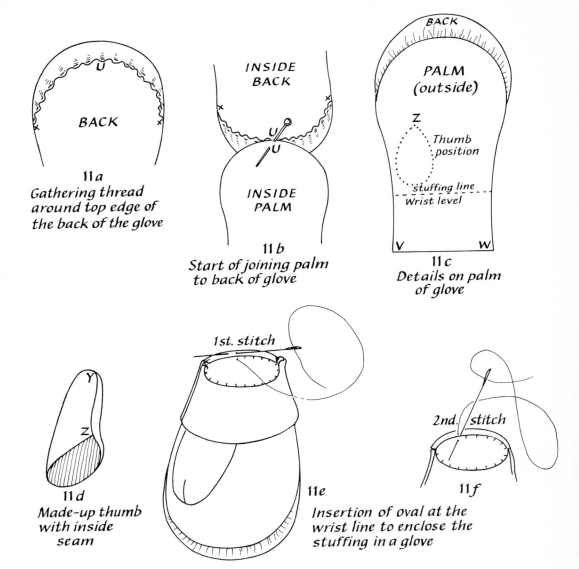

11a
Gathering thread
around top edge of
the back of the glove

11b
Start of joining palm
to back of glove

11c
Details on palm
of glove

11d
Made-up thumb
with inside
seam

11e

11f

Insertion of oval at the
wrist line to enclose the
stuffing in a glove

9. *THE BOXING GLOVES* (*Diagram 11a–e*)

Make up each glove as follows:

a. Sew in the gathering thread on the back of the gloves, with small running stitches near the edge of the felt between x . . . x. Pull up the thread to curve the top well over the palm. Leave the end to adjust the gathers later (see Diagram 11a).

b. Place U on the palm piece to U on the back, with right sides together (Diagram 11b). Pin at U, V and W and where the gathers begin and end. Adjust the gathers to fit the palm and back of the glove evenly together.

c. Keeping the gathers uppermost, work a double oversewn seam (see page 15) along the gathered section, making a stitch over and between each gather.

d. Continue the seam to the cuff edge with back-stitch, and then close the seam on the other side of the palm from the gathers to the cuff in the same way.

e. Turn the glove right side out (Diagram 11c). Retain the curved over top by filling it with one firm *roll* of stuffing, and then stuff to the dotted line at wrist level.

f. The thumbs. Fold the thumb in half and double oversew an inside seam from Y to Z (Diagram 11d). Turn it right side out and with the rounded end of a stuffing stick or similar object, push out the top of the thumb from the inside in order to well round its shape.

g. Next stuff the thumb firmly, leaving the base of it to be completely filled when it is partly sewn on to the palm.

h. Attach the thumb to the palm by placing Z on the thumb to Z on the palm (see Diagrams 11c and 11d), and fitting the bottom edge to the dotted line indicated on the palm pattern. Ladder-stitch this seam securely, adding the final filling to well stuff the thumb before closing it completely.

Remember to reverse the position of the thumb on the second glove to make a pair.

i. To keep the stuffing in the gloves, turn the cuffs back to the wrist line and stitch the small oval of felt round the wrist line into the thickness of the glove felt (Diagrams 11e and 11f).

j. Turn down the cuff and sew the centre of a very narrow piece of tape approximately 9 inches long to the back of the wrist and when the glove is secured to the sleeve this is wound round and tied—boxing glove style. Attach the gloves later to the completed costume.

10. *THE WHITE GLOVES* (*Diagrams 12a–c*)

(These can be made as an alternative to the Boxing Gloves.)
First check that all the glove pieces are cut out exactly the same size and shape, and that the finger slits are the same lengths as given on the pattern.

a. Beginning and ending at the cuff edges pin the glove pieces evenly together to form a pair and finely oversew very near the edges of the felt.
b. The fingers and thumbs are stiffened to allow them to be placed in various positions. For each one cut a $2\frac{1}{2}$–3 inch piece of pipe cleaner and turn back $\frac{1}{4}$ inch of each end of wire on itself to prevent damage (Diagram 12a). Fold each piece of pipe cleaner near its centre and insert the folded ends into the fingers and thumbs, varying the position of the wire ends to avoid too much bulk in one place (Diagram 12b).
c. Lightly stuff the palm of each glove with soft filling to the wrist only.

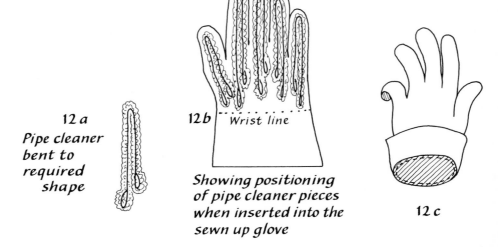

12 a
Pipe cleaner bent to required shape

12b Wrist line

Showing positioning of pipe cleaner pieces when inserted into the sewn up glove

12 c

d. To keep the filling in place, turn the cuffs back over the gloves and sew the oval wrist felts in position inside each glove round the wrist lines (without showing stitches on the outside). (Diagram 11e, 11f, and 12c.)

11. MAKE UP OF TUNIC AND TROUSERS

$\frac{1}{4}$ yard of gaily figured 36 inch material is required for the tunic.
12 in. × 18 in. of striped or plain material for the trousers with its bodice.

Cottons are very suitable but other light weight materials could be selected.
Trace and cut out the five patterns on pages 144–146 using greaseproof paper.
Note that the turnings for the shoulders and round the armholes are narrower than the other seams as these will be bound with bias binding. $\frac{3}{8}$ inch is allowed elsewhere for the French seams (see page 19).

The tunic
   a. Fold sufficient material lengthways through the centre of the design and place and pin the centre front edge of the pattern to the fold. Pin round the pattern and cut out along the *edge* of the paper (which will allow for the turnings as shown).
   b. The pair of sleeves are cut on double material, folded so that the design is placed centrally on both sleeves. Pin the pattern to the material and cut out as above (a).
   c. Close the sides of the tunic with French seams (see page 19) but do not close the shoulders at present.
   d. Fold up and neatly stitch the $\frac{1}{2}$ inch hem.
   e. Next place the trouser patterns for the front and the back on the folded material. Pin and cut out as directed for the tunic.
   f. Cut the slit across the back along the line given on the pattern and bind these edges with bias binding. Mitre the corners to make the ends neat and strong.
   g. Pin and sew the sides and the seams between the legs as French seams —keeping the seam very narrow at the top of the slit. Turn up each trouser leg and stitch a $\frac{1}{2}$ inch hem as invisibly as possible. Press all the seams and hems on the tunic and trousers and turn both garments right sides out.

h. Place the tunic over the bodice of the trousers so that now both garments can be made up as one. Tack the two garments together round each armhole. Fold in the $\frac{1}{4}$ inch turnings along the neck front and back of the trouser bodice and tunic, with the raw edges between the two garments. Oversew the two folded edges together.

i. Each sleeve is attached to the double bodice *before* the sleeve seams are closed. It will be noticed that the insertion of the sleeve is inverted as compared with normal tailoring, to accommodate the upward positions of the little finger and thumb used in the sleeves to manipulate the puppet. Verify which sleeve is used for each armhole. (Refer to the pattern and Diagram 13 for this and the stages of work round the armhole.) Keeping the right sides of the materials together and the sleeve uppermost, place and pin the sleeve to the armhole at A B and C (1 in Diagram 13).

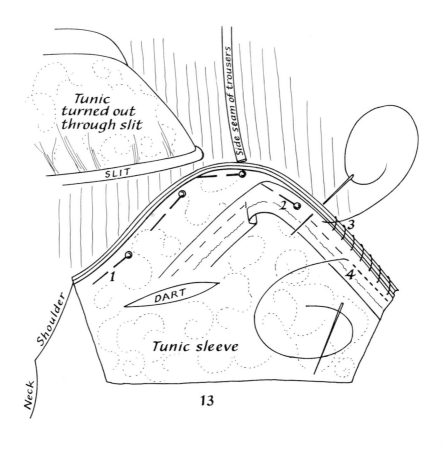

13

j. Open one turning of the thin bias binding and include this with the
¼ inch turnings round the armhole keeping all four raw edges level (2 in
Diagram 13).

k. Oversew the four raw edges together (as at 3) and then back-stitch the
armhole seam along the fold on the binding, forming a ¼ inch seam (4).
To complete the binding, fold it closely over the raw edges and hem
to the back—stitching along the other side of the turnings.

l. Back-stitch the dart as shown on the sleeve pattern.

m. Diagram 14 shows the closing of the shoulder and sleeve seams. Fold
the sleeve as shown, placing E to E at the hem line. A/B exactly together
to close the armhole and D to D at the neckline. Attach thin bias binding and close this seam from D to E in the same way as round the
armhole. Turn up the cuff edge and stitch a ¼ inch hem. Attach the
second sleeve to its armhole in the same manner.

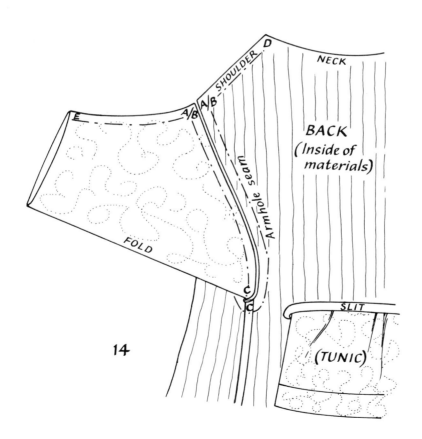

12. ASSEMBLING THE PARTS

To attach each glove (Diagram 15)

a. Turn back the cuff over the glove to the oval felt at the wrist line. Place and pin the left glove to the left arm with the seam nearest the thumb, level with the sleeve seam.

b. Ladder-stitch the fold of the hem of the sleeve to the wrist line inside the glove, making $\frac{1}{8}$ inch stitches in the glove felt and approximately $\frac{1}{4}$ inch stitches in the hem, to take up the extra width of the sleeve and create a little fullness.

c. Turn down the cuff (and tie the tapes of the boxing gloves if these have been chosen).

To attach the legs (Diagram 16)

Insert the left leg into the appropriate trouser leg and pin the top of each felt leg along the stitch line, level with the top of the leg slit. On the right side stitch through the four thicknesses of material across each trouser leg.

To attach the head

Centralize the front and back head seams with the centre front and back of the costume, pin the neck edge of the completed garment to just cover the edge of the finger-stall circle on the base of the head. Ladder-stitch together.

13. THE RUFF (*Diagram 17a and b*)

This will require a piece of white Tarlatan or similar stiffened material, $27\frac{1}{4}$ inches long by 3 inches wide.

a. Fold the material lengthways about $\frac{1}{4}$ inch to one side of the centre and well crease this fold, then open it flat again.

b. Pencil spot the positions of the pleats along the line of the fold at the regular intervals marked on the pattern.

c. Follow the instructions and fold and pin the pleats inwards and outwards to create box pleats. Stitch each fold in place along the line of dots.

d. Stitch an 18 inch length of narrow ribbon or Russia braid along the

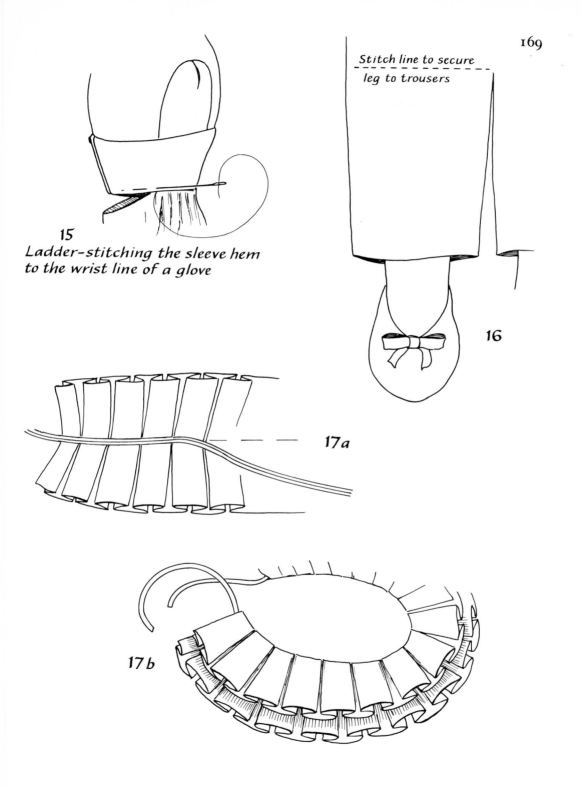

15
Ladder-stitching the sleeve hem
to the wrist line of a glove

Stitch line to secure
leg to trousers

169

16

17a

17b

stitch line, leaving sufficient at each end to make a bow to close the ruff round the neck (Diagram 17a).

e. Fold the pleating along the ribbon to cover it, keeping the narrower side on top of the wider one (Diagram 17b). Place the ruff round the Clown's neck and tie the braid or ribbon at the back.

THE CLOWN'S BALL

Cut 8 pieces of different coloured felts from the ball pattern given on page 146. Pin and stab-stitch each section to the next until the last seam only remains. Stuff the ball with soft filling mixed with foam chippings and then close the last seam. Stitch a 6 inch piece of round or very narrow elastic to one end of the ball and sew an inch loop at the other end. Pass this over the Clown's hand to fit tightly round the wrist. This ball also can be used with the animal puppets.

The Teddy Bear Family

Mr. and Mrs. Bear, Betty and Bernie

Teddies, as glove puppets in the two sizes given to form a family unit, will provide endless entertainment. Either of the two smaller puppets can be duplicated to add to the family. Colours can be changed to various shades of brown, to white or gold and can then become 'friends' of the family. The adult bears can also be altered in the same way. Varying the costumes and accessories will provide further contrasts.

It will be noted that two shapes for the heads are used—one for the females and another for the male bears. It is important to place the features accurately. The position of eyes are usually at a lower level in the head of the youngsters and proportionately the ears are larger and wider apart than on the adults. Observing these details will improve the appearance and give more character to them when used as puppets or as toys. Cheerful expressions are sometimes difficult to obtain unless the mouth marks are accurately formed. A drooping mouth line produces a doleful character, so curve the mouth line upwards at the corners for happy Bears!

MATERIALS

To make the family of four puppets shown in the photograph on page 173 using the same fur fabric for each, the following is required:

$\frac{1}{2}$ yd. × 48 in. fawn fur fabric (wool or nylon) for the heads, legs and paws. (The pile stroking in the 18 in. direction.) In addition, for each puppet's body and garments, etc., the following is needed:

Mr. Bear   9 in. × 21 in. dark brown felt.

        1 oz. 3 ply knitting wool for pullover in one or more colours and No. 11 needles.

        6 in. × 15 in. scarlet felt for jacket.

        A pair of 13 mm. brown glass eyes.

Mrs. Bear   12 in. × 9 in. fawn felt.

12 in. × 16 in. turquoise felt for coat and shoulder bag.

7 in. × 30 in. striped cotton material for dress.

A pair of 13 mm. brown glass eyes.

Betty Bear   5 in. × 13 in. oyster felt.

6 in. × 16½ in. patterned cotton material for dress.

A pair of 11 mm. brown glass eyes.

Bernie Bear 6 in. × 16 in. gold felt.

8 in. × 13½ in. coloured or striped cotton for shirt.

A pair of 11 mm. brown glass eyes.

All bears will need dark brown Anchor soft embroidery cotton for mouth marks, etc., and a mixture of rayon filling and woodwool for stuffing.

To make each bear in separate colours the following amounts of fur fabric are required for the heads, arms, legs and paws.

Mr. Bear   12 in. × 17 in. (Chart 9)

Mrs. Bear   12 in. × 18 in. (Chart 2)

(Pile stroking in the 12 inch direction)

Bernie Bear   12 in. × 12 in. (Chart 12)

Betty Bear   13 in. × 13 in. (Chart 6)

The felt and cotton materials together with the other items were given in the first list.

GENERAL INFORMATION (*for all four Bears*)

No turnings are required on the felt pieces unless stated to the contrary. Allow ¼ inch turnings on the fur fabrics beyond the marking out lines round the templates. For the cotton garments the turnings are shown on the pattern pieces.

The inside seams on the felt should be open back-stitched very near the edges. The inside seams for the fur fabrics are open back-stitched just inside the marking out line. Other details of stitching, etc., are given on pages 13–19. Except for coloured tacking use self-coloured thread throughout.

Make the card templates from the patterns on pages 174–189 and as instructed on page 26. Perforate the position lines by piercing them with a thick needle, through which a pencil point can be used in marking out.

(*Continued on page 201*)

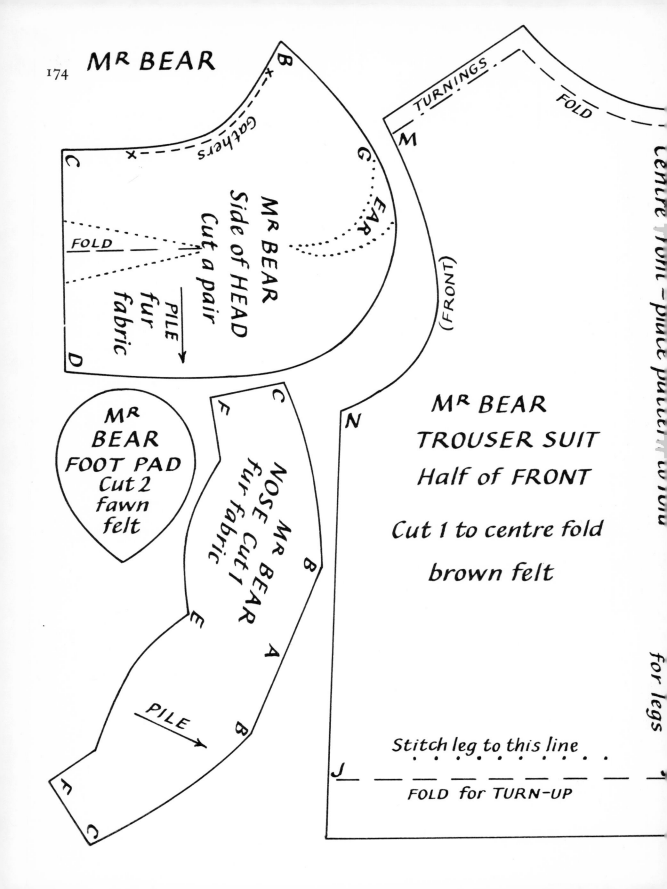

MR BEAR

174

B

x----Gathers

x

C

MR BEAR
Side of HEAD
Cut a pair

G
EAR

FOLD

PILE
fur
fabric

D

MR
BEAR
FOOT PAD
Cut 2
fawn
felt

C
F

NOSE
MR BEAR
fur Cut 1
fabric

B

E

PILE

A

B

F

C

TURNINGS

M

FOLD

centre front — place pattern to fold

(FRONT)

N

MR BEAR

TROUSER SUIT

Half of FRONT

Cut 1 to centre fold

brown felt

for legs

Stitch leg to this line . . . .

J

FOLD for TURN-UP

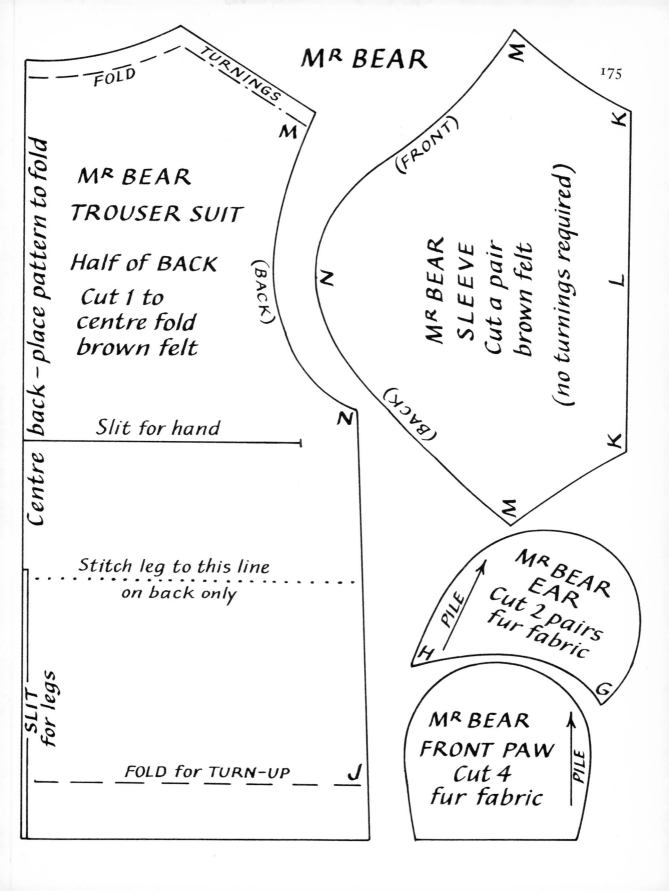

MR BEAR

MR BEAR TROUSER SUIT

Half of BACK

Cut 1 to centre fold brown felt

FOLD

TURNINGS.

M

Centre back – place pattern to fold

(BACK)

N

Slit for hand

N

Stitch leg to this line on back only

SLIT for legs

FOLD for TURN-UP

J

MR BEAR SLEEVE Cut a pair brown felt

(FRONT)

(BACK)

M

K

L

(no turnings required)

K

M

MR BEAR EAR Cut 2 pairs fur fabric

PILE

H

G

MR BEAR FRONT PAW Cut 4 fur fabric

PILE

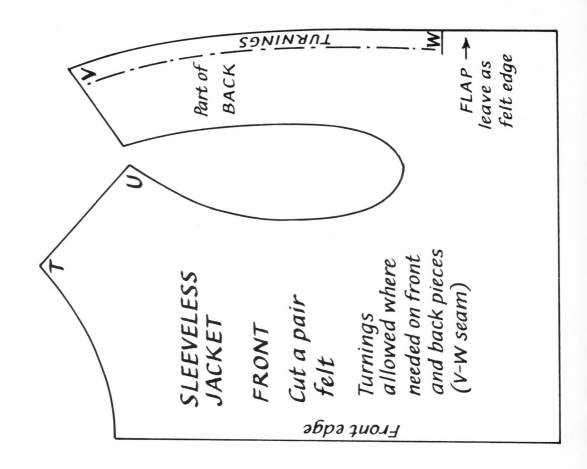

Part of BACK

TURNINGS

W

FLAP → leave as felt edge

V

U

T

SLEEVELESS JACKET

FRONT

Cut a pair felt

Turnings allowed where needed on front and back pieces (V-W seam)

Front edge

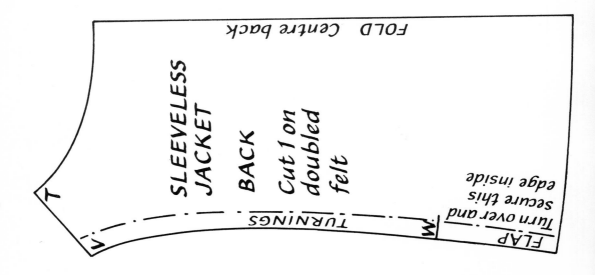

FOLD Centre back

SLEEVELESS JACKET

BACK

Cut 1 on doubled felt

T

V

TURNINGS

W

Turn over and secure this edge inside

FLAP

Mr and Mrs BEAR

17

NOSE
Cut 1
leather
DART DART

**MRS BEAR
FOOT PAD
Cut 2
oyster
felt**

D (BACK) D

**MR BEAR
HEAD GUSSET
Cut 1
fur fabric**

PILE

(EAR)   (EAR)

(FRONT)

B   A   B

**WRIST
OVAL
Cut 2
felt**

MR and MRS
BEAR

**MR BEAR
FRONT
PAW PAD
Cut 2
fawn felt**

**MRS BEAR
EAR
Cut 4
fur fabric**

PILE

TURNINGS IN SLIT

L   M

Stuffing line

**MR and MRS BEAR
LEG and PAW**

Cut 2 for each
with dart
Cut 2 for each
without the dart

fur fabric

PILE

DART
FOLD

N

**MRS BEAR
FRONT
PAW PAD
Cut 2
oyster felt**

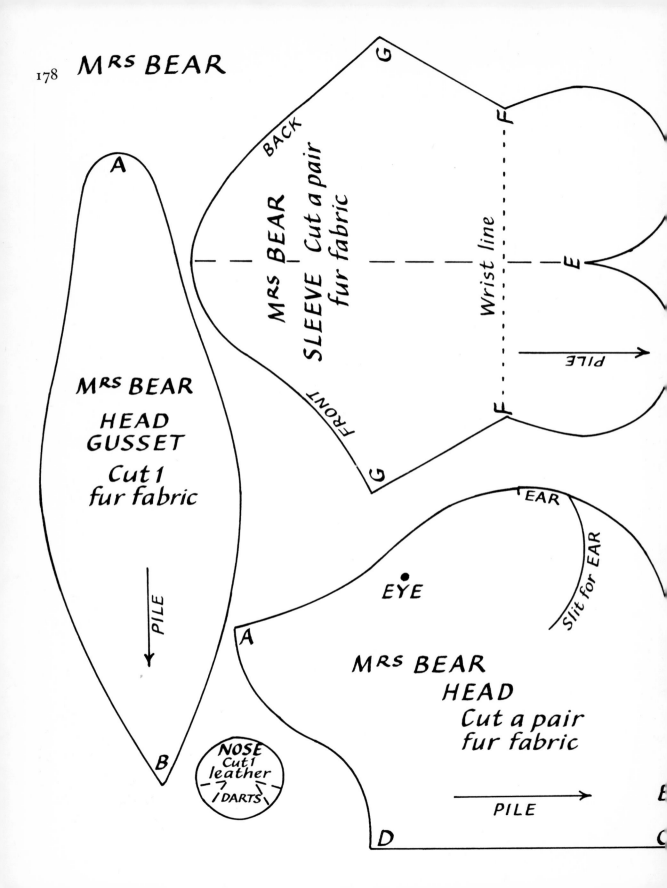

M^{RS} BEAR

G

F

BACK

M^{RS} BEAR SLEEVE Cut a pair fur fabric

Wrist line

E

PILE

F

F

A

M^{RS} BEAR

HEAD GUSSET

Cut 1 fur fabric

PILE

G

G

EAR

Slit for EAR

EYE

A

M^{RS} BEAR

HEAD

Cut a pair fur fabric

B

NOSE Cut 1 leather

DARTS

PILE

D

C

MRS BEAR

FRONT FLAP
MRS BEAR'S BAG
— — FOLD — —
Cut 1 felt
BACK TOP
× Stitch to gathered edge ×

MRS BEAR'S BAG
FRONT TOP
Cut 1 felt
× Stitch to gathered edge ×

Gathers
MRS BEAR'S
SHOULDER BAG
felt
Cut 1 back, and 1 front
and stab-stitch to-
gether along base

Cut 1 STRAP 8 ins. long felt

TURNINGS

FOLD OF MATERIAL CENTRE BACK

Fold for inverted pleat

Fold for inverted pleat

Vertical stripes

MRS BEAR

DRESS (striped cotton)

SKIRT BACK
(half pattern)
Cut 1 on double
material

Hem line

FOLD

FOLD

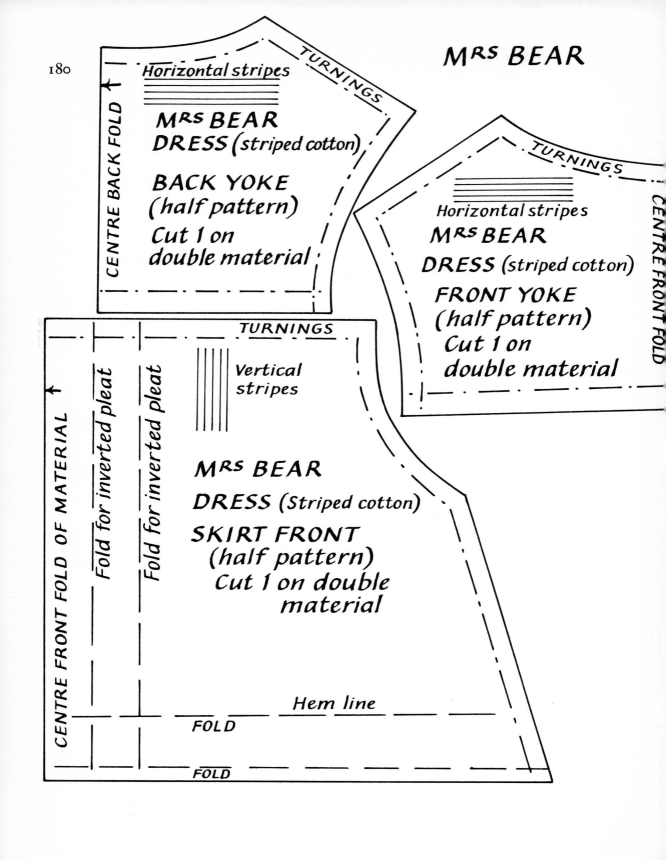

MRS BEAR

Horizontal stripes

MRS BEAR
DRESS (_striped cotton_)

BACK YOKE
(_half pattern_)
Cut 1 on
double material

CENTRE BACK FOLD

TURNINGS

Horizontal stripes

MRS BEAR
DRESS (_striped cotton_)

FRONT YOKE
(_half pattern_)
Cut 1 on
double material

CENTRE FRONT FOLD

TURNINGS

TURNINGS

_Vertical
stripes_

MRS BEAR

DRESS (_Striped cotton_)

SKIRT FRONT
(_half pattern_)
Cut 1 on double
material

Fold for inverted pleat

Fold for inverted pleat

CENTRE FRONT FOLD OF MATERIAL

Hem line

FOLD

FOLD

MRS BEAR

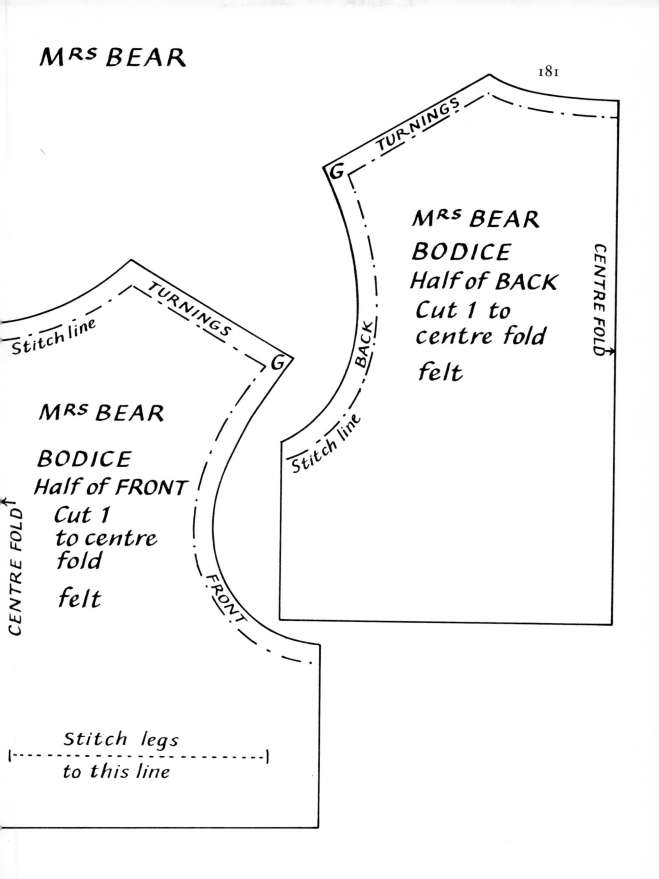

TURNINGS

G

MRS BEAR
BODICE
Half of BACK
Cut 1 to
centre fold
felt

CENTRE FOLD →

BACK

Stitch line

Stitch line

TURNINGS

G

MRS BEAR

BODICE
Half of FRONT
Cut 1
to centre
fold
felt

CENTRE FOLD ↑

FRONT

Stitch legs
to this line

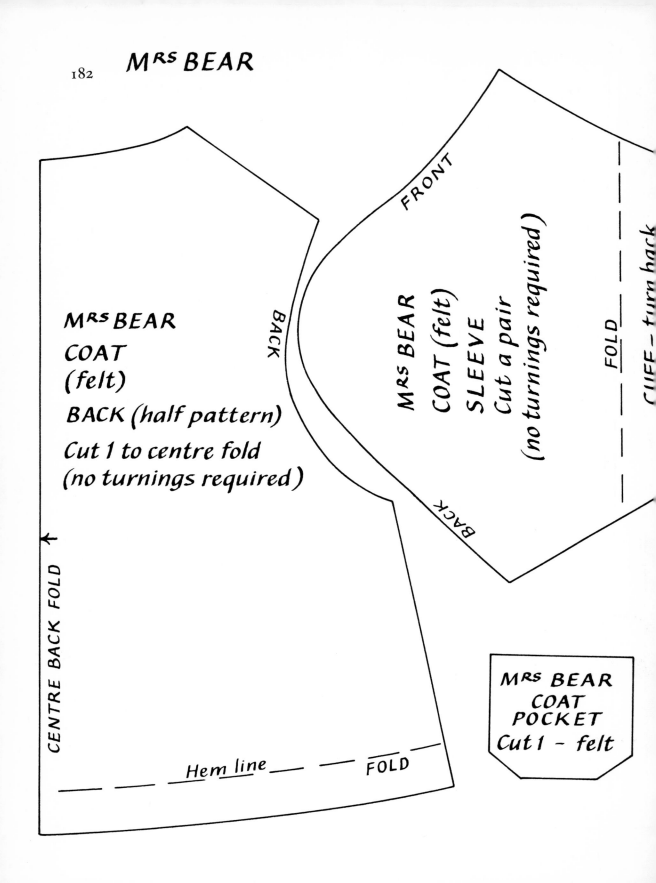

MRS BEAR

MRS BEAR
COAT
(felt)
BACK (half pattern)
Cut 1 to centre fold
(no turnings required)

CENTRE BACK FOLD

Hem line — — — FOLD

FRONT

BACK

MRS BEAR
COAT (felt)
SLEEVE
Cut a pair
(no turnings required)

FOLD

CUFF – turn back

BACK

MRS BEAR
COAT
POCKET
Cut 1 – felt

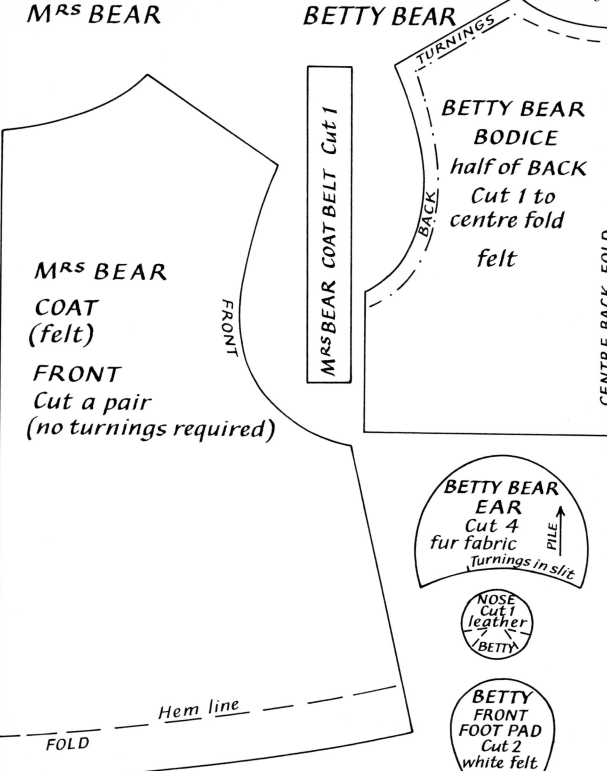

MRS BEAR

BETTY BEAR

MRS BEAR COAT BELT Cut 1

BETTY BEAR
BODICE
half of BACK
Cut 1 to
centre fold
felt

TURNINGS

BACK

CENTRE BACK FOLD

MRS BEAR
COAT
(felt)
FRONT
Cut a pair
(no turnings required)

FRONT

BETTY BEAR
EAR
Cut 4
fur fabric
PILE
Turnings in slit

NOSE
Cut 1
leather
BETTY

BETTY
FRONT
FOOT PAD
Cut 2
white felt

Hem line

FOLD

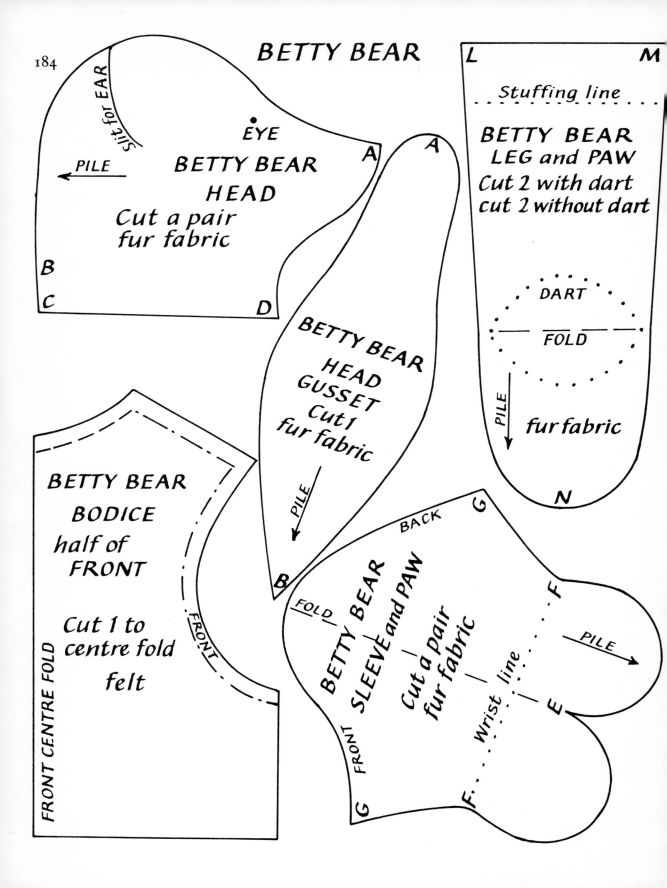

184

BETTY BEAR

Slit for EAR

PILE

EYE

BETTY BEAR
HEAD
Cut a pair
fur fabric

A

B

C

D

A

BETTY BEAR
HEAD
GUSSET
Cut 1
fur fabric

PILE

B

L

M

Stuffing line

BETTY BEAR
LEG and PAW
Cut 2 with dart
cut 2 without dart

DART

FOLD

PILE

fur fabric

N

BETTY BEAR
BODICE
half of
FRONT

Cut 1 to
centre fold
felt

FRONT CENTRE FOLD

FRONT

BACK

G

FOLD

BETTY BEAR
SLEEVE and PAW

Cut a pair
fur fabric

FRONT

G

F

PILE

Wrist line

E

F

BETTY BEAR

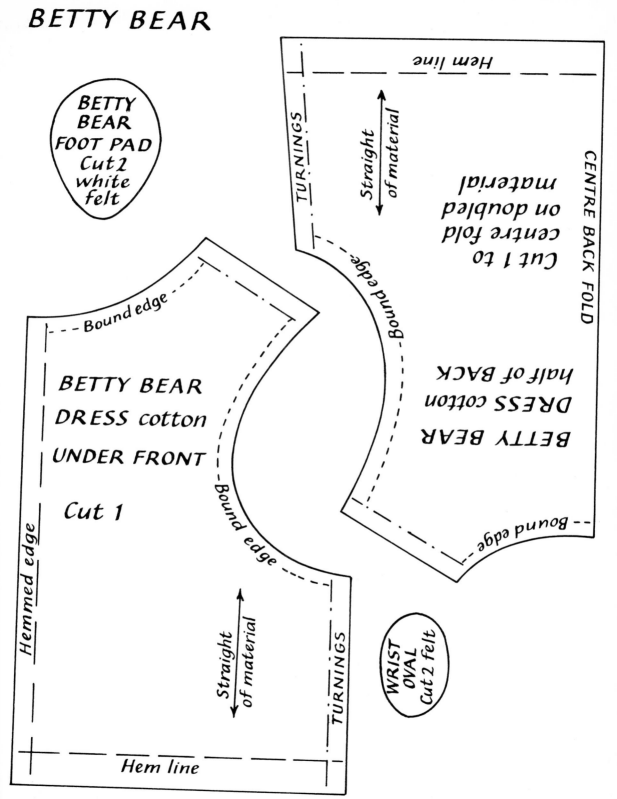

BETTY BEAR FOOT PAD Cut 2 white felt

Hem line

TURNINGS

Straight of material

CENTRE BACK FOLD

Cut 1 to centre fold on doubled material

BETTY BEAR DRESS cotton half of BACK

Bound edge

Bound edge

BETTY BEAR DRESS cotton UNDER FRONT

Cut 1

Bound edge

Bound edge

Hemmed edge

Straight of material

TURNINGS

WRIST OVAL Cut 2 felt

Hem line

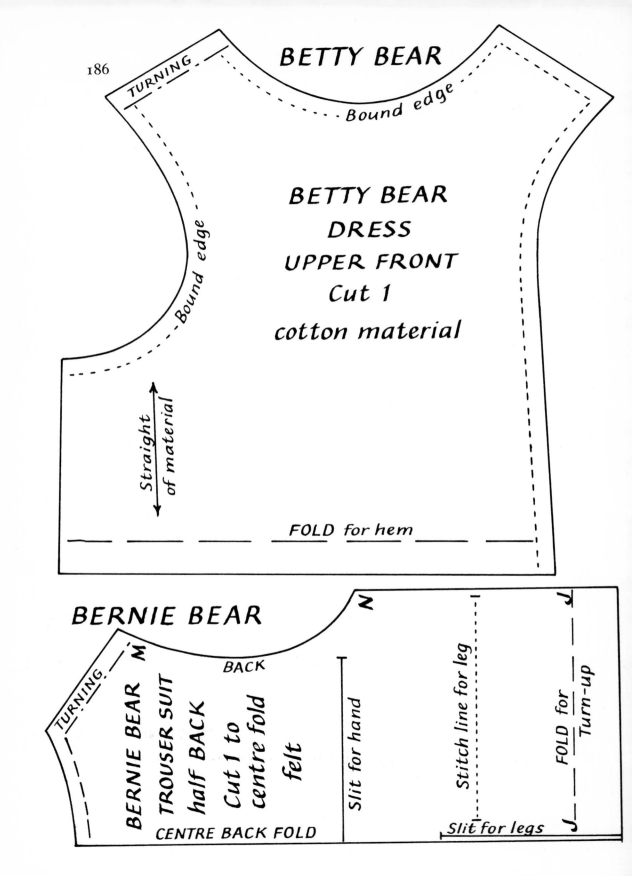

BETTY BEAR

TURNING

Bound edge

Bound edge

**BETTY BEAR
DRESS
UPPER FRONT
Cut 1

cotton material**

Straight
of material

FOLD for hem

BERNIE BEAR

TURNING.

M

N

BACK

BERNIE BEAR
TROUSER SUIT
half BACK
Cut 1 to
centre fold
felt

Slit for hand

Stitch line for leg

FOLD for
Turn-up

CENTRE BACK FOLD

Slit for legs

BERNIE BEAR

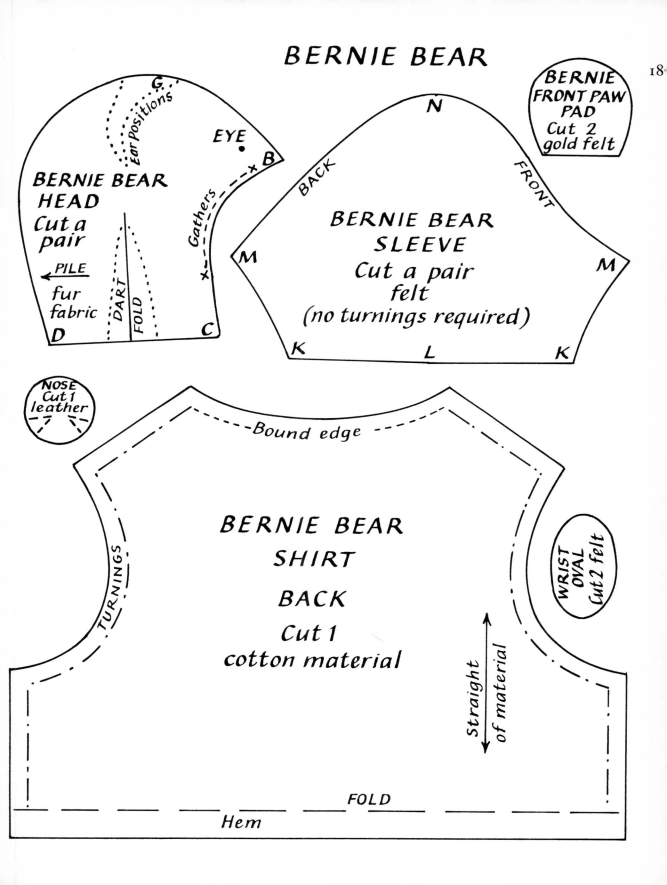

18

BERNIE FRONT PAW PAD Cut 2 gold felt

G

Ear positions

EYE

B

BERNIE BEAR HEAD Cut a pair

← PILE

fur fabric

Gathers

DART

FOLD

D

C

BERNIE BEAR SLEEVE Cut a pair felt (no turnings required)

N

BACK

FRONT

M

M

K

L

K

NOSE Cut 1 leather

—Bound edge—

BERNIE BEAR SHIRT BACK Cut 1 cotton material

TURNINGS

WRIST OVAL Cut 2 felt

Straight of material

FOLD

Hem

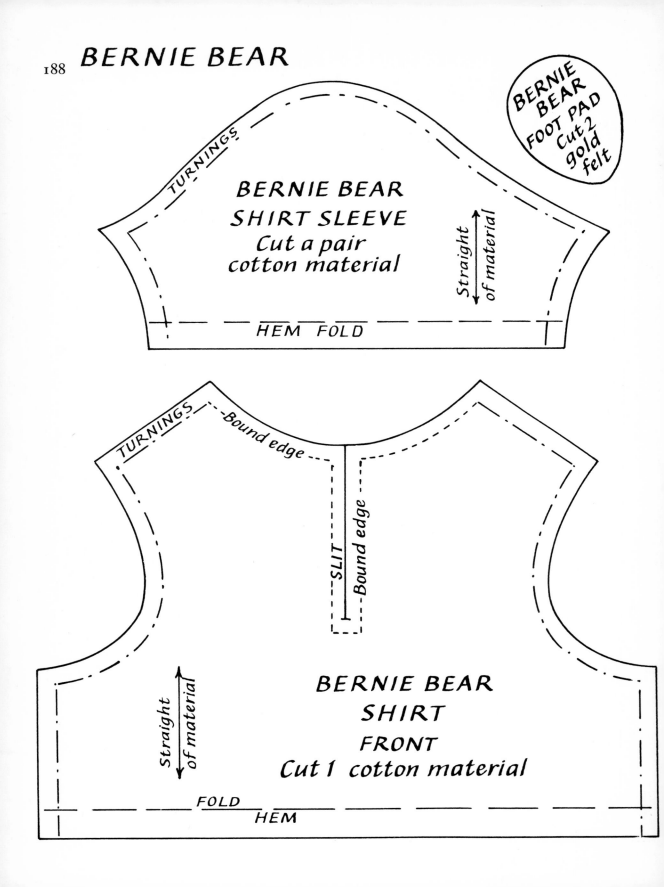

BERNIE
BEAR
FOOT PAD
Cut 2
gold
felt

TURNINGS

BERNIE BEAR
SHIRT SLEEVE
Cut a pair
cotton material

Straight
of material

HEM   FOLD

TURNINGS

Bound edge

SLIT

Bound edge

Straight
of material

BERNIE BEAR
SHIRT
FRONT
Cut 1 cotton material

FOLD

HEM

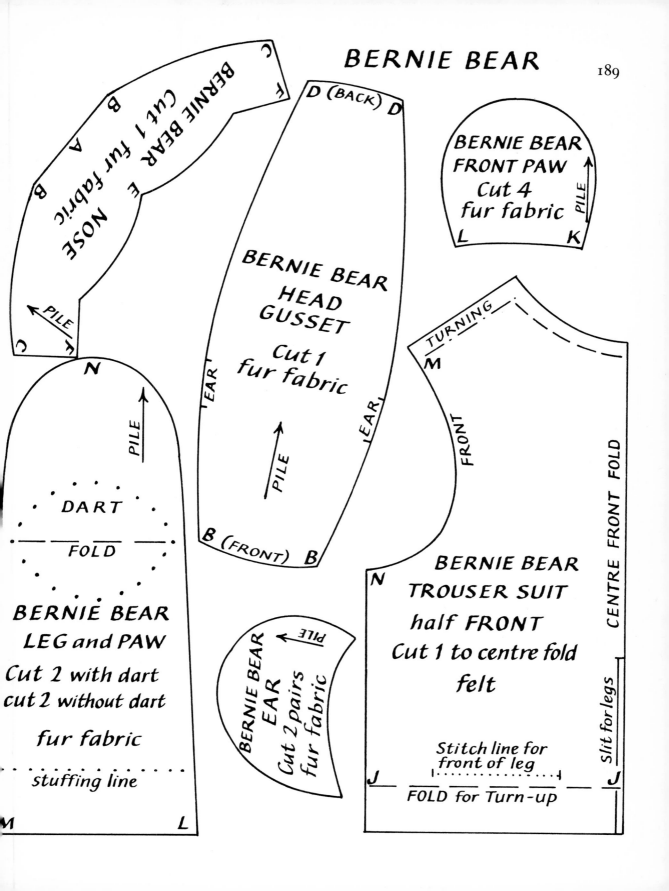

BERNIE BEAR

189

BERNIE BEAR
Cut 1 fur fabric

BERNIE BEAR
Cut 1 fur fabric

NOSE

PILE

BERNIE BEAR
HEAD
GUSSET

Cut 1
fur fabric

PILE

EAR

EAR

B (FRONT) B

BERNIE BEAR
FRONT PAW
Cut 4
fur fabric

PILE

D (BACK) D

TURNING

FRONT

CENTRE FRONT FOLD

PILE

DART

FOLD

BERNIE BEAR
LEG and PAW

Cut 2 with dart
cut 2 without dart

fur fabric

stuffing line

BERNIE BEAR
EAR
Cut 2 pairs
fur fabric

PILE

BERNIE BEAR
TROUSER SUIT
half FRONT
Cut 1 to centre fold
felt

Stitch line for
front of leg

FOLD for Turn-up

Slit for legs

Chart 1
Fur fabric
48″ × 18″
for the Bear
Family

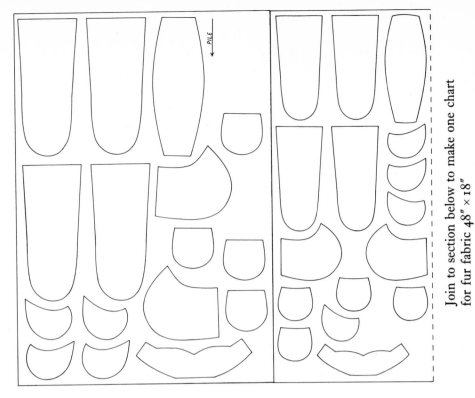

PILE

Join to section below to make one chart
for fur fabric 48″ × 18″

Mr. Bear   18″ × 12″   Bernie Bear   18″ × 7½″

Join section above to this line

PILE

Mrs. Bear   18″ × 13″   Betty Bear   18″ × 8½″

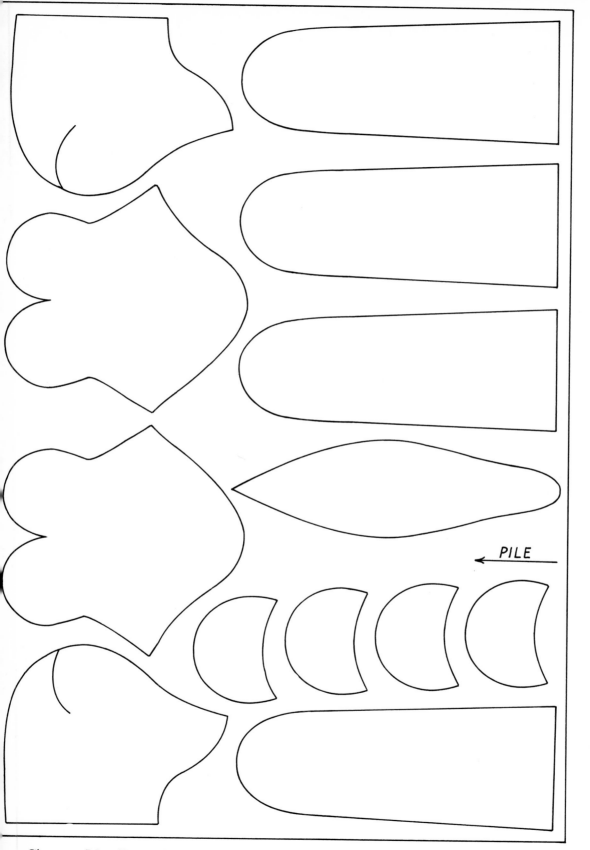

PILE

Chart 2   Mrs. Bear   Arms, Head & Legs fur fabric   12″ × 18″

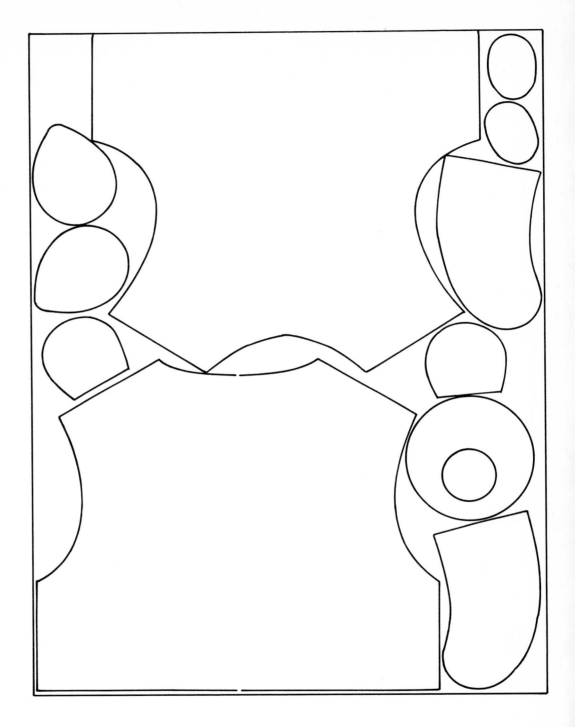

Chart 3   Mrs. Bear   Fawn felt Bodice Pads and Stall   12″ × 9″

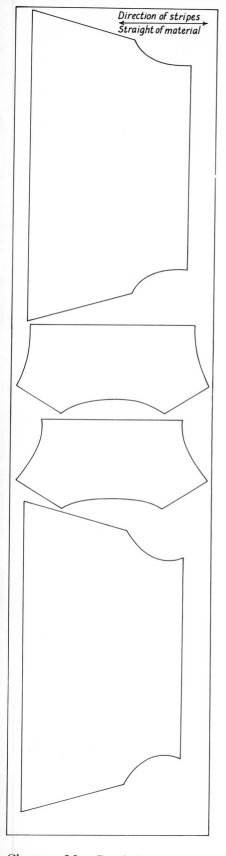

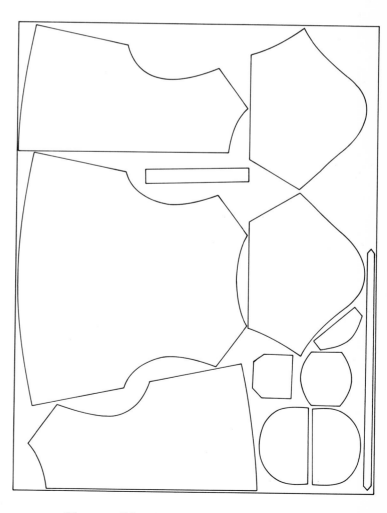

Chart 4   Mrs. Bear's Dress   30″ × 7″

Chart 5   Mrs. Bear's Coat and Bag   Felt   16″ × 12″

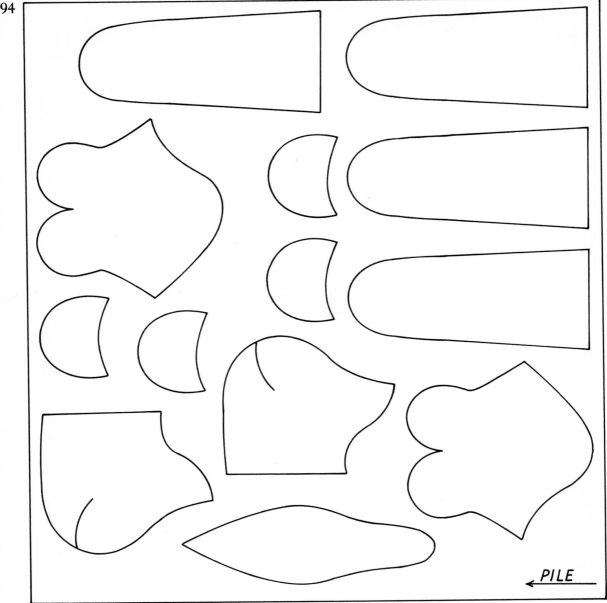

PILE

Chart 6   Betty Bear   Fur fabric. Head, legs and arms $13'' \times 13''$

Chart 7   Betty Bear. Bodice Oyster felt   5″ × 13″   Chart 8   Betty Bear's Cotton Dress   6″ × 16½″

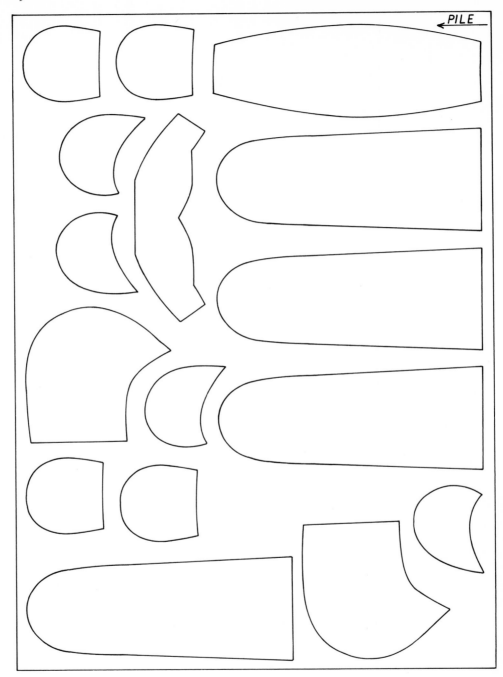

PILE

Chart 9 Mr. Bear. Head and Legs. Fur fabric 12″ × 17″

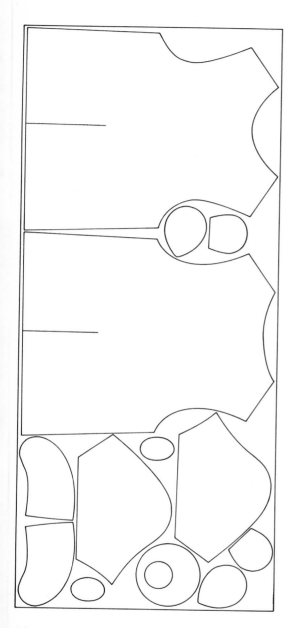

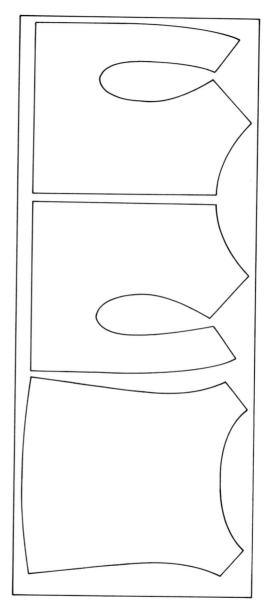

Chart 10   Mr. Bear. Trouser Suit
Dark brown felt   9″ × 21″

Chart 11   Mr. Bear's Jacket
Scarlet felt   15″ × 6″

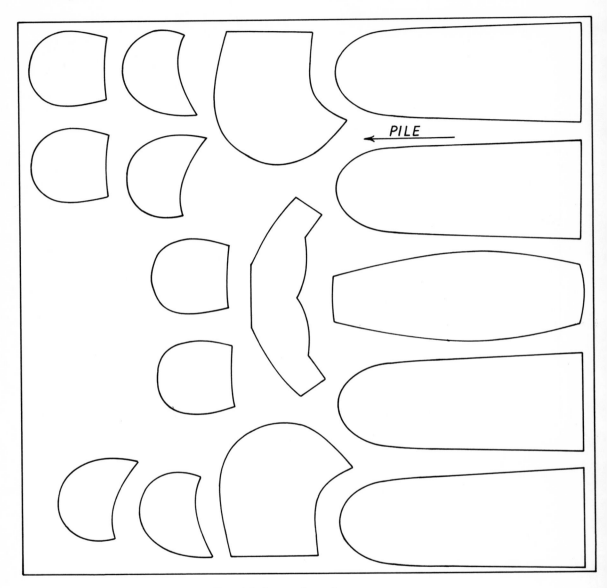

PILE

Chart 12   Bernie Bear   Fur fabric   12″ × 12′

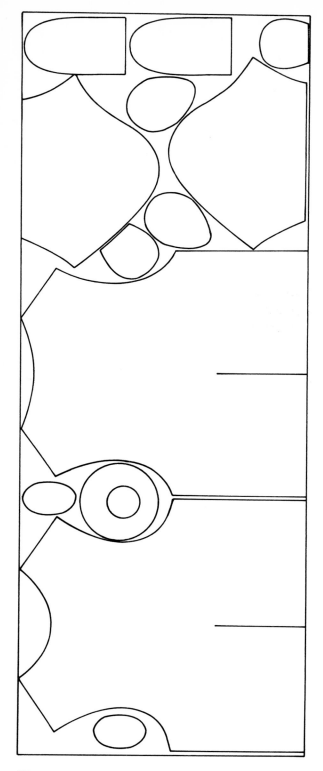

Chart 13 Bernie Bear Trouser
Suit Gold felt 16″ × 6″

Stripes

Chart 14   Bernie Bear   Cotton Shirt   8″ × 13½″

If all the bears are to be made up in the same material, place the templates for the fur fabric on the back of the material, as shown on Chart 1 observing the arrows for the direction of the pile and allowing $\frac{1}{4}$ inch turnings. Follow individual charts if Bears are to be made up in different fur fabrics.

Mark and cut out as instructed on page 27. Sew coloured tacking along the position lines which have to be seen on the outside of the fabric (for eyes, mouth marks, ears, etc.) using a contrasting thread. See page 16.

Mark and cut out the felt pieces in the various colours following the information on page 27. Place the templates on the felts as given on the Charts concerned.

Information for the cotton garments is given on the pattern pieces.

Betty Bear is a smaller version of Mrs. Bear and is made up from the same instructions but is dressed differently.

Bernie Bear is the smaller design of Mr. Bear and has the same instructions but has his own clothes.

Some of the garments will have to be put on and taken off over the legs and not over the heads which are usually too large for the neck openings.

MRS. BEAR AND BETTY BEAR

1. The head

   a. Place two ear pieces, right sides together. Pin at each base corner first, then round the top, pushing the pile inwards along the edges (Diagram 1a). Open back-stitch the seam (just on the inner side of the marking out line) but not across the base.

MRS BEAR and BETTY BEAR

1a   Ear pinned and seam
for inside seam

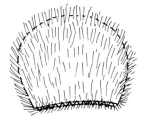

1b   Ear. Oversewn base
edge on outside

b. Turn the ear right side out, lift any pile caught in the seam to get the full thickness of the pile on the edge of the ear.

c. Oversew the raw edges together across the base of the ear (without turning them inwards) (Diagram 1b).

d. Make up the second ear in the same way.

e. To insert each ear cut the slits on the two head pieces exactly where marked (Diagram 1c). Working on the inside of each head piece, insert two thirds of the base of each ear into the slit and pin securely in position allowing $\frac{1}{4}$ inch turnings on the base of the ear and $\frac{1}{8}$ inch on the slit edges (Diagram 1d). Sew up the slit with stabbed back-stitch. The remaining part of the ear base is brought forward towards the nose and pinned to the head turning (Diagram 1e). The three thicknesses should be oversewn together to keep them in place ready for the head seam.

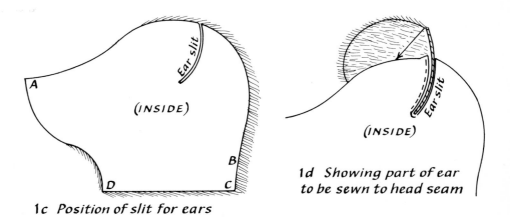

1c Position of slit for ears

1d Showing part of ear to be sewn to head seam

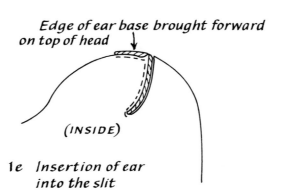

Edge of ear base brought forward on top of head

1e Insertion of ear into the slit

f. Insert the second ear in exactly the same way.

g. *Insertion of the head gusset.* With right sides of the fur fabric together, insert a threaded needle through A on the gusset and then through the corner of the marking out line at A on a head piece (Diagram 2a). Pull the thread through the two fabrics and make two small stitches on the spot to secure them firmly together. Attach the second head piece to the gusset in the same way. This should ensure that the gusset is in the centre.

h. Pin the head pieces evenly to the gusset on both sides first at B and then between, including the sections of the ears brought forward from the slits. See that the sides are level with no bias to twist the gusset. Starting at A, back-stitch both seams, stabbing the stitching over the four thicknesses at the ears.

i. After the second seam reaches B continue to C (Diagram 2b). (The head can be turned to check the evenness of the gusset before closing the front seam.)

j. Pin and stitch the front of head seam A to D.

k. Turn the head right side out and lift any pile caught in the seams so that they are as invisible as possible. Fold up the $\frac{1}{4}$ inch turnings round the neck edge and tack them invisibly in place.

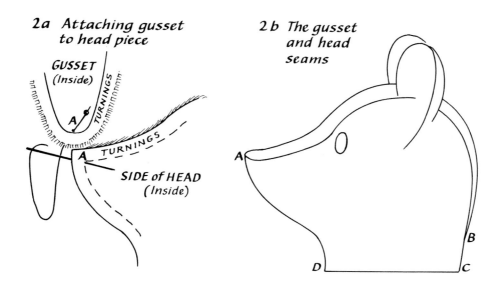

2a *Attaching gusset to head piece*

GUSSET (Inside)

TURNINGS

A

A TURNINGS

SIDE of HEAD (Inside)

2b *The gusset and head seams*

A

D   B

C

2. Stuffing the head

Follow the instructions for making and using cushions of rayon and wood-wool mixed as given on page 29. Lightly fill the neck until the finger-stall has been inserted, when the stuffing can be completed.

3. The finger-stall

Refer to page 37 to make the finger-stall, using No. 6 for Mrs. Bear and No. 7 for Betty Bear. For the insertion of the finger-stall see page 39.

4. The features

a. *The nose* is made from a piece of brown or black soft gloving leather or felt. Mark round the template on the back of the material and cut out exactly to size. (If preferred hold the pattern on the material firmly and cut out round it.)

Fold the darts (x over y) where indicated in Diagram 3a and stitch each dart in place at the edge only. Stick a little knob of stuffing to the back of the nosepiece and then pin it in position. Do not sew it to the head before the mouth marks are worked.

b. *The mouth marks* are formed using a double long darning needle and brown Anchor soft embroidery cotton. Insert the needle in the right eye position, and bring it out in the centre of the nose (Diagram 3b) leaving the knotted end in the eye position. Make a chain stitch in front of the nose (Diagram 3c) and then take the needle through to the left to start the mouth line as shown in Diagram 3d and marked by coloured tacking. Take the needle and thread across the front, passing under the final part of the chain stitch and insert the needle on the right side of the mouth at the same distance and level as on the left side (Diagram 3e). Take the needle and thread out through the left eye position and end off securely. (The start and end of the thread will be covered by the eyes.)

c. Hem the nose to the head as invisibly as possible keeping it even and centred. The completed mouth and nose are shown in Diagram 3f including the curved up corners for a happy expression. Sagging mouths never smile.

d. *Preparation and Insertion of the Eyes* (wire type).

Follow the instructions for Method II given on page 22 for forward facing eyes on white felt circles. Place them at the positions already

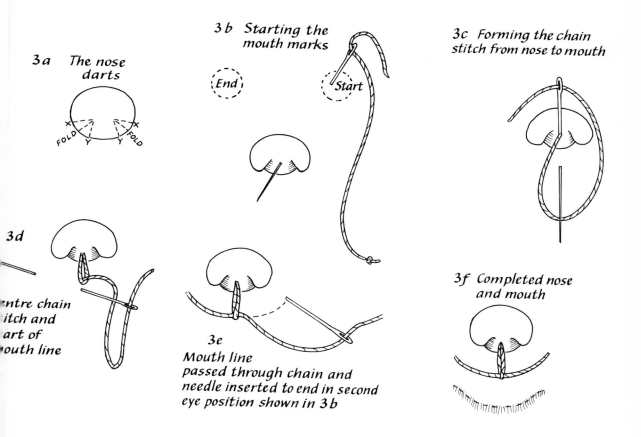

3a The nose darts

FOLD × × FOLD

3b Starting the mouth marks

End ⌐ ⌐ Start

3c Forming the chain stitch from nose to mouth

3d

ntre chain
itch and
art of
outh line

3e Mouth line passed through chain and needle inserted to end in second eye position shown in 3b

3f Completed nose and mouth

marked by the coloured tacking, and insert them as shown on page 24.

e. The fur fabric round the nose and mouth may need a little even clipping with a comb and scissors if a long pile fabric has been used. Do not overdo this to show the foundation of the fabric.

5. The felt bodice and fur fabric sleeves (Mrs. Bear and Betty)

To make up each fur fabric sleeve:

a. Sew in coloured tacks (see page 16) along the wrist line to indicate the position of the wrist oval.

b. Fold the sleeve in half along the fold line, right sides together. Starting at E pin and back-stitch the paw and sleeve seam. (Oversewing the seam until the full $\frac{1}{4}$ inch turnings are reached to secure the tapered raw edges.)

c. Turn the sleeve and paw right side out, then fold the sleeve back over the paw to the wristline.

d. Stuff the paw with soft filling and oversew the wrist oval along the coloured tacking line round the wrist to enclose the stuffing. Remove the tacking and turn the sleeve back to be right side out.

e. Make up the second sleeve in the same manner.

f. *The tunic bodice*—$\frac{1}{4}$ inch turnings are needed round the neck, armholes and across the shoulders as shown on the pattern, but not on the side seams. First join the front and back pieces at the side seams, back-stitching on the inside very near the edge.

g. Back-stitch across the shoulders allowing $\frac{1}{4}$ inch turnings.

h. Fold down the neck edge turnings and tack to the inside of the bodice.

i. *To insert the fur fabric sleeves.* With the bodice inside out and the sleeves right sides out, place each sleeve inside the bodice with the front edge of the sleeves to the front of the bodice (Diagram 4). Pin in position so that each sleeve seam is a continuation of the shoulder seam. (The sleeves are inverted as compared with a normal garment to facilitate the movement of the fingers in working the puppet.) Back-stitch the armhole seams allowing $\frac{1}{4}$ inch turning on the felt and fur fabric. To neaten the turnings they can either be oversewn or finished bound with a bias binding.

j. The base edge of the tunic can be trimmed with a narrow lace edging as a feminine finish. This should be attached by back-stitching just inside the felt edge and the lace eased as it is sewn on (Diagram 5).

6. *The legs*

Two pieces of fur fabric are required for each leg, one with the large dart for the front of the ankle to bring up the foot to a level position.
To make each leg:

a. Place the front and back leg pieces, right sides together and pin them together at L and M. Pin also at the centre front at N and between these points at frequent intervals, keeping both sides even. Back-stitch from L to N to M.

b. Fold the dart along the centre, then pin as shown in Diagram 6 and back-stitch along the dotted curved line.

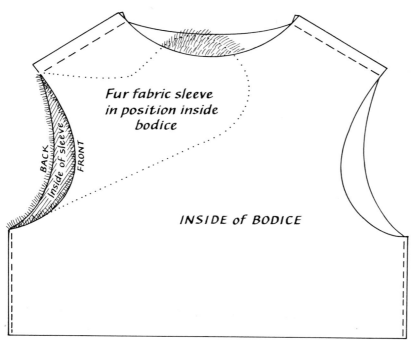

4 Showing position of a sleeve inside the bodice, ready
to sew into the armhole

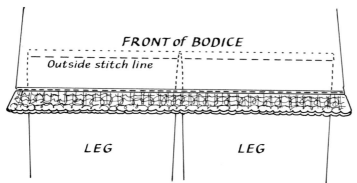

5 Lace edging attached to the base edge of felt
bodice. The dotted lines indicate positions of
the legs inside the base of the bodice. Detached
lines indicate the back-stitching to attach each
leg to the front of the bodice only

    c. Sew in the coloured tacking across the stuffing line.

    d. Fold in the $\frac{1}{4}$ inch turnings at the top of the leg and tack them down invisibly. Turn the leg right side out.

    e. Stuff the foot with soft filling then fill the leg as a separate section to get a good bend at the ankle dart. Insert the filling up to the stuffing line, ending with much less filling to taper off the thickness. No filling is needed above the stuffing line.

    f. Close the top of the leg with oversewing or ladder-stitching.

    g. Place each leg in position under the tunic—the top of the leg level with the stitch line as shown on the pattern, and in Diagram 5. With the tunic uppermost, back-stitch along the stitch line taking up one thickness of fur fabric only with the felt, to secure the front of the leg to the tunic. The back of the tunic is not attached to the leg but left open for the insertion of the hand to work the puppet.

7. *To attach the head to the body*

The neck edge should have been folded inside already and tacked in place.

    a. Pin the neck edge of the tunic to the head just outside the finger-stall circle to cover the stitching. First pin the centre front and back and then at the shoulders.

    b. Ladder-stitch the fold round the neck to the head. Two rows of stitching are recommended to be really secure (see page 17).

8. *Paw marks and pads (Diagram 7)*

Using dark brown Anchor soft embroidery cotton, make four large stitches over the front seam of each back and front paw, spacing them evenly to represent the divisions of the toes. Start and end the thread where it will be covered by the felt pad. Attach the felt pads by pinning them in a central position on the paws and hemming them securely to the fur fabric.

9. *Mrs. Bear's dress (Diagram 8)*

Patterns for cotton materials are best made in greaseproof paper. The seams can either be machined or worked by hand. In both cases they should be small and finely worked.

    Turnings and other information are given on the pattern pieces, which should be noted as the garment is made up.

6
The leg dart folded for stitching along the curved line

7
The attachment of felt for pads and large stitches indicating division of toes

8 *Mrs Bear's Striped Dress*
Centre front length 6 ins.
The back is the same style but without the braid trimming. It fastens on the shoulders

a. Place the pattern pieces on striped material as shown in Chart 4, and pin in position. Cut out along the edge of the pattern.
b. Fold and tack down the centre front and centre back inverted pleats as indicated on the pattern.
c. Place and pin the base of the front yoke over the top of the front skirt, right sides together. Tack and sew across the bodice on the stitch line. Repeat to attach the back yoke to the skirt.
d. To finish the edges of the armholes and the neck, use a thin bias binding from which one of the folded edges is removed to reduce its width (Diagram 9). Attach it as instructed on page 19.
e. To close the shoulder openings, sew two very small press studs to each shoulder, placing the front over the back edges.

10. Mrs. Bear's coat (Diagram 10) (Chart 5)

This coat is made up in turquoise felt with inside seams back-stitched very near the edges of the felt as no turnings are allowed.

a. Place a front piece to each side of the back, right sides together and back-stitch the side and shoulder seams.
b. Fold each sleeve right sides together and stitch the seams, omitting the last $\frac{1}{2}$ inch at the cuff edge. Turn the sleeves and stitch the seam at the cuff on the outside, which, when the cuff is turned up, will not show.
c. Insert and pin each sleeve into its correct armhole in the same way as given in Diagram 4. Back-stitch round the armhole near the edges.
d. The coat can be trimmed to individual taste, but the coat given has a pocket, a belt at the back and is trimmed at the neck with a thick wool lampshade braid sewn flat to the neckline. It is fastened with a hook and eye at the neck.

11. The shoulder bag

This optional extra is made up from a simple design. See Diagrams 11a and 11b and the instructions on the pattern. First stab-stitch the front and back pieces together round the curved base. Insert a separate gathering thread along each piece and back-stitch the base of the tops to the gathered edge. Attach the 8 inch strap handle to the back of the bag. Fasten with a press stud or very small button.

FOLD

Turning cut away   Cut edge

9

*Bias binding showing
one folded turning cut
away to make binding
narrower*

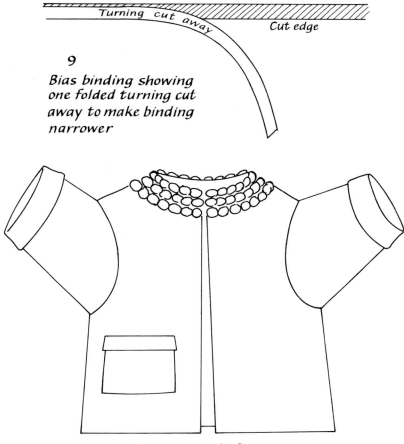

10 *Mrs Bear's Coat*
felt with wool braid neck trimming

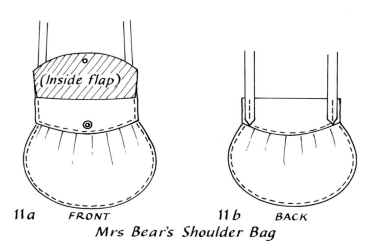

11a FRONT   *11b* BACK

Mrs Bear's Shoulder Bag

12 Betty Bear's Dress. Made in a small patterned cotton with bound edges in the main colour. Shoulder fastening

12. Betty's dress (Diagram 12)

Choose a small pattern material such as one suitable for a child's dress. Place and pin the greaseproof paper pattern to the material as shown on Chart 8. Cut out exactly to the edge of the pattern. The turnings are allowed as indicated. Edges without turnings are bound using a thin bias binding in the main colour. Reduce its width by removing one turning and refold the edge.

a. Stitch the side seams and shoulders as French seams (see page 19).
b. Fold and stitch a $\frac{1}{8}$ inch hem up the centre edge of the under front.
c. Turn up and invisibly stitch the hem along the base of the dress.
d. Bind the armholes (see page 19) and then bind the remaining edges starting at the top of the front under section.
e. The shoulder can be fastened with two small press studs, placing the front edge over the back.

MR. BEAR AND BERNIE

First read the points given above under General Information for all the bears.

1. The head

  a. Sew in the coloured tackings along the lines as given on the pattern for the ear positions. Close the dart on each head piece by folding this section in half as indicated and back-stitch along the marking out line.

  b. Pin A on the head gusset to A at the centre front of the nose piece (Diagram 2a page 203). Back-stitch the inside seam B A B across the middle of the face.

  c. Sew in the gathering thread between x . . . x on the two head pieces, sewing along the marking out line. Adjust the gathers to fit B C on the head to B C on the nose piece. (It is easier to measure this using the nose piece pattern.) End the threads and pin and stitch the seams B C joining the head to the nose on each side of the face.

  d. Following Diagram 13, pin the back of the head gusset to the head pieces D to D and then pin at 1 inch intervals from B to D keeping the edges even. Back-stitch both seams from B to D.

  e. Pin and back-stitch the front seam E F. Fold back the $\frac{1}{4}$ inch turnings round the base of the head and invisibly tack them in place.

  f. Turn the head right side out and lift any pile caught in the seams.

2. Stuffing the head

Instructions for making and using cushions of rayon and woodwool fillings are given on page 29. Lightly fill the neck until the finger-stall has been inserted, when the neck stuffing is completed.

3. The ears

To make each ear:

  a. Place a pair of ear pieces, right sides together and pin at each corner, then round the ear, pushing in the pile along the edge (see Diagram 1a on page 201). Back-stitch the ear seam but not across the base.

  b. Fold back the base turnings and invisibly tack them in place, keeping the front and back edges separate.

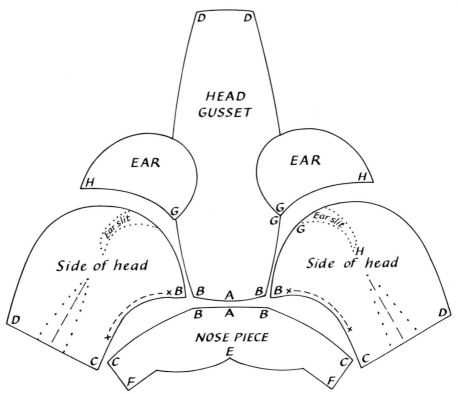

13 *Showing the relative positions of the head pattern pieces*

c. Turn the ear and lift any pile caught in the seams.

d. *To attach the ears*. Place and pin the ears in position G to G and H to H (as shown on Diagram 13), following the coloured tacking on each head piece. Pin both ends of the ears to the ends of the tacking. Attach the front of the ear first, ladder-stitching into the fold of the turnings and just outside the coloured tack line, then secure the back of the ear. Use strong thread and start and end securely.

4. *The finger-stall and insertion*. Using pattern No. 5 for Mr. Bear and No. 7 for Bernie, follow the instructions for the make up of the stall on page 37 and the insertion on page 39.

5. *The features.*   Follow the instructions given for Mrs. Bear, Section 5, a–f.

6. *The body and trousers (or trouser suit)* (Chart 10 for Mr. Bear and Chart 13 for Bernie Bear)

This is made up in felt as one piece. No turnings are needed except where given on the shoulder seams and round the neck.

a. Place the front and back pieces, right sides together. Starting at J on each side seam, pin and back-stitch near the edge of the felt. Then pin and sew the inner leg seams from J to J. The four short parts of the seams beyond J are sewn on the reverse side to avoid an outside seam on the turn-ups.

b. Pin and sew the shoulder seams leaving $\frac{1}{4}$ inch turnings.

c. Pin and back-stitch the seam for the sleeves. Fold up an $\frac{1}{8}$ inch of felt at the wrist edge, and tack in place.

d. Make up each paw in the same way as the ears (Section 3a, b and c above).

e. Stuff the paws lightly. Oversew the wrist ovals to the folded edge of the paws to enclose the filling.

f. Turn the sleeves right sides out and attach the paws by securely ladder-stitching through the folded sleeve edges to the outside of the over-sewing round the ovals (K L K).

g. Keeping the trouser suit inside out and the sleeves right sides out, place the appropriate sleeve in an inverted position, inside the bodice so that the back and the front edges of the sleeves and the bodice lie evenly together (see Diagram 4). Pin the sleeves evenly into the armholes and then back-stitch round them near the edges of the felt.

h. Turn the garment right sides out. Fold in and tack down the $\frac{1}{4}$ inch turnings round the neck. Fold up the turn-ups.

i. Cut the slit across the back in the position marked on the pattern. Fold in $\frac{1}{8}$ inch along each edge and using matching thread, work a close back-stitch on the outside as near the fold as possible. Closely oversew the ends of the slit.

7. *The Legs*

Make up each leg as for Mrs. Bear, Section 6 and attach them to the line indicated on the *back* of the trouser suit.

8. To attach the head. Follow the instructions given for Mrs. Bear on page 210, section 7a and 7b.

9. Paw marks and pads. See page 208, section 8 for Mrs. Bear.

10. Mr. Bear's knitted pullover

Use a pair of No. 11 needles and 1 oz. of 3 ply wool in two colours, for the striped pullover shown in the photograph—turquoise and scarlet. (Alternatively the two main colours, if Mr. Bear is one of a group of dressed bears.)

Except for the ribbing of knit 1, purl 1 the pullover is worked in stocking stitch.

   a. *The front.* Cast on 56 stitches, and work 6 rows of ribbing.

      Work 4 rows of stocking stitch.

      Change to the second colour for the next 4 rows (and for each alternate 4 rows as the work progresses).

      Start the base of the armhole by decreasing 2 stitches at the beginning of the next two rows and then continue decreasing one stitch at each end of each row until 32 stitches remain (12 rows).

      Continue for 22 rows on the 32 stitches, ending on a purl row.

      Knit 12, cast off 10 for the neck. Knit 12.

      Continue on the last 12 stitches for 6 rows, and cast off.

      Return to the 12 stitches left on the needle, re-join the wool and knit 6 rows. Cast off.

   b. *The back.* Work the back decreasing as for the front until 24 rows of stocking stitch has been completed above the ribbing, leaving 32 stitches.

      To divide for the centre back opening, work half-way across a knit row and cast on 2 stitches to form the lap-over for the fastening. (These 2 stitches should be worked as knit stitches in the purl rows.)

      Continue on this half of the back for 16 rows, ending with a knit row.

      Cast off 8 stitches for the neck and continue on the remaining 10 stitches for 8 rows. Cast off.

      Join the wool for the other half of the back and complete as for the first half, adding 2 stitches for the overlap for the centre opening.

   c. *The ribbed neck.* Pick up 52 stitches and work ribbing for 12 rows. Cast off loosely.

d. *The striped sleeves.* For each, cast on 40 stitches and work in ribbing for 12 rows.

Work in stocking stitch for 8 rows. Cast off 2 at each end of the next row.

Work 12 rows of striped stocking-stitch, decreasing 1 stitch at each end of every knit row until 12 stitches remain. Cast off.

Using wool, close the side, shoulder and sleeve seams and insert the sleeves into the armholes, placing the seam as a continuation of the shoulder seam to invert the position of the sleeve, necessary for a puppet.

Fasten the back opening with press studs.

11. Mr. Bear's sleeveless felt jacket (Chart 11)

This jacket is given as an alternative to the knitwear. Cut out the back and the pair of front pieces, following the instructions on the pattern.

a. Working on the outside of the jacket, fold in the $\frac{1}{4}$ inch turnings along the seams V W on the back and place each folded edge over the turnings down the V W edge on the front pieces for a lapped seam. Back-stitch or machine stitch the seams on the outside, near the folded edge, leaving the lower part of each seam open, as for the flap of a hacking jacket. Secure the flap turnings.

b. On the inside of the garment, back-stitch the shoulder seams near the edges of the felt for an inside seam without turnings.

c. Attach a narrow, fancy or Russia braid round the armholes, neck and on the front edges. Start and end at the front of the neck, leaving sufficient braid to tie a bow to fasten the jacket.

12. Shirt for Bernie

This garment is attractive in a narrow stripe material. Place and pin the pattern pieces as shown on Chart 14. Do not allow turnings as they are included where necessary as indicated.

a. Pin the back and front pieces together and stitch the side seams and shoulders as French seams (see page 19).

b. Fold up the turnings round the base and invisibly hem or machine in place.

c. Fold up and hem or machine the cuff edges and close each sleeve with a French seam.

d. Turn the sleeves right sides out. Place each sleeve in an inverted position inside the bodice and pin to the appropriate armhole as marked on the pattern pieces and in Diagram 4. Pin and back-stitch the sleeves to the armholes keeping the shoulder and sleeve seams as a continuous seam.

e. With a thin bias binding (made narrower by removing one turning and refolding the edge) bind the neck and front opening (see page 19). Close the shirt with a small hook and eye. If preferred a white collar can be made and attached to the neck, or the neck and front opening can be finished with a facing and turned back as revers.